Eternal

Christianity

Systematic Annihilationism:
Is The Bad News Essential? Did Christ By His Sacrifice Prevail Upon God To Infinitely Pardon Us? Was Jesus Beast Or God? Is Dr. John Stott An Evangelical?
Jim Cronfel

Lama Sabachthani?
A Sermon Delivered On Lord's-day Morning, March 2nd, 1890, by Rev. C. H. SPURGEON, At The Metropolitan Tabernacle, Newington

Psychopannychia
OR, A REFUTATION OF THE ERROR ENTERTAINED BY SOME UNSKILFUL PERSONS, WHO IGNORANTLY IMAGINE THAT IN THE INTERVAL BETWEEN DEATH AND THE JUDGMENT THE SOUL SLEEPS. TOGETHER WITH AN EXPLANATION OF THE CONDITION AND LIFE OF THE SOUL AFTER THIS PRESENT LIFE.
John Calvin

Jim Cronfel

Copyright © 2006   Jim Cronfel

ISBN: 1-933899-43-3

Published by:
Holy Fire Publishing
Unit 116
1525-D Old Trolley Rd.
Summerville, SC 29485
www.ChristianPublish.com

Cover Design: Jay Cookingham

Printed in the United States of America and the United Kingdom

Soli Deo Gloria

"Then whosoever heareth the sound of the trumpet, and taketh not warning; if the sword come, and take him away, his blood shall be upon his own head. He heard the sound of the trumpet, and took not warning; his blood shall be upon him. But he that taketh warning shall deliver his soul"
(Ezekiel 33:4-5).

.

Table of Contents

PREFACE

Jim Cronfel believes "conversion comes from the awareness of eternal conscious torment," that "[Christianity] is about fleeing hell and sin." Annihilationists believe that even the consideration of a literal, eternal hell is intolerable and "the fire and brimstone school of theology" not to be "biblical Christianity."

Jim Cronfel believes conversion comes from the awareness of eternal conscious torment, that [Christianity] is about fleeing hell and sin. Yet, Annihilationists believe that even the consideration of a literal, eternal hell is intolerable and the fire and brimstone school of theology is not biblical Christianity. Yet there are many that promote this belief like Dr. John Stott who was named Time magazine's "100 most influential people in the world" and was recognized by Rev. Billy Graham as "the most respected clergyman in the world today. Cronfel's worthy goal in his book, "Eternal Christianity" is not to tear down honored gentlemen but to boldly exalt the name of Jesus Christ and proclaim what He eternally accomplished for us on Calvary.

Cronfel urges his readers to carefully examine the Scriptures that show the eternal fear of God must precede an authentic gospel conversion. He finds it troubling that annihilationism pervades bestsellers like "Basic Christianity" and "The Cross of Christ." Cronfel aims to show how one unbiblical view leads to a series of others which could lead to denying God himself. For support, he includes Spurgeon's "Lama Sabachthani," a sermon about Christ's eternal cry from the Cross; and, Calvin's tract "Psychopannychia," which means "the imaginary sleep of the soul."

Cronfel points out when Dr. Stott wrote that there would be "a serious disproportion between sins consciously committed in time and torment consciously experienced throughout eternity," he rejected original sin. Therefore, there would be a serious disproportion between "good deeds" consciously committed in time and "grace" consciously experienced throughout eternity.

Annihilation theology denies that God punished Jesus for our sins. However, evangelical Christians believe Christ's substitutionary punishment for sins is the central tenant of their faith. Cronfel goes on in his book to address other issues like the deity of Christ and forgiveness as it relates to annihilationism and proves prove that people still need to repent in fear of the true hell.

Annihilationsim is so controversial that Cronfel lost membership at Armitage Baptist Church in Chicago for opposing it. "Eternal Christianity," including Cronfel, Spurgeon and Calvin and is available at Amazon.com and bookstores. Also, Cronfel's testimony and conversion during a pizza delivery set to music, "The Episode," will be available as a digital download or on CD at Amazon.com. He can be contacted at eternalchristianity@yahoo.com

Acknowledgements

Thanks to my pastors, teachers and friends: Augustine, Anselm, Luther, Calvin, WGT Shedd, John Gerstner, Michael Horton, John Armstrong, R.C. Sproul, Chuck Ellis, Carl Haak, Barry Muraff, John Robbins, Hank Hanegraaf, Gary Almy and Benny Hinn; and, my precious few supporters amidst the onslaught of persecution (by some on this list) against my cross. And, thank you to Dr. John Stott and IVP for allowing me to proceed. And, also, thank you to the U.S. of A., Mom and Dad, Holy Fire Publishing and my editors. God save us!

Jim Cronfel
Chicago, 2006

Systematic Annihilationism:
Is The Bad News Essential? Did Christ By His Sacrifice Prevail Upon God To Infinitely Pardon Us? Was Jesus Beast Or God? Is Dr. John Stott An Evangelical?

Jim Cronfel

I.   INTRODUCTION TO DR. JOHN R. W. STOTT

In the October 5, 1998 edition of *Christianity Today* magazine, in "Is Hell Forever?"[1] one Linda Piepenbrink asked if evangelical theologians accepted annihilationism. Professor Stanley J. Grenz from Regent College explained that annihilationism is the belief that hell is the soul's burning up into non-existence. He defended eternal conscious torment, that hell is forever, but he did not claim that annihilationists attack original sin and atonement. He defended Dr. John R.W. Stott as being an accepted annihilationist by evangelical theologians even though Dr. Stott rejects justification by faith alone.

But annihilationism violates original sin, where eternal conscious torment comes from, and is rank unrepentance. Justification by faith alone is impossible if the atonement is not also defined by eternal conscious torment. This is not a direct discussion of "weeping and gnashing of teeth" or "the worm that dieth not" or hell per se. We will be discussing the Law and the gospel, not hell. This is about wrath and righteousness.

Dr. John Stott is very famous. In the November 2004 edition of the *New York Times*, editor David Brooks said that Dr. Stott was a more likeable evangelical than Jerry Falwell or Pat Robertson.

> It is a voice that is friendly, courteous and natural. It is humble and self-critical, but also confident, joyful and optimistic. Stott's mission is to pierce through all the encrustations and share direct contact with Jesus. Stott says that the central message of the gospel is not the teachings of Jesus, but Jesus himself, the human/divine figure. He is always bringing people back to the concrete reality of Jesus' life and sacrifice.[2]

---

[1] Stanley J. Grenz, "Is Hell Forever?" Christianity Today (October 5, 1998), 92

[2] David Brooks, "Who Is John Stott?" *The New York Times*, (November 30, 2004)

Dr. Stott is one of *Time* magazine's "100 most influential people" in the world in 2005. His books have been translated into over 100 different languages. He is the honorary Chairman of the Lausanne Committee for World Evangelization. He is one of the editors of *Christianity Today* magazine. He has honorary PhD's in three separate countries. The Queen of England appointed him "the Commander of the British Empire," and he teaches Bible study to President Bush. Rev. Billy Graham says that he is "the most respected clergyman in the world today." His assistant writes about his humility in *Christianity Today*.

> I had learned a key characteristic of Dr. Stott: his disarming humility. Dr. Stott turns 80 years old on April 27. Known principally for his writing (almost 40 books) and preaching, Dr. Stott has been one of the most influential leaders of world evangelicalism in the last 50 years. Much has been written about Dr. Stott's theology and his influence on evangelicalism worldwide, with little attention paid to his personal life.[3]

This book also pays attention to his theology, not his personal life. I have been more faithful to him than his own assistant and publisher and fans. I am focusing on original sin, not slander and gossip. Original sin applies equally to all mankind. My quotes are from his theological works that he invites the public to scrutinize and debate. I insist that you buy Dr. Stott's books: *The Cross of Christ, Basic Christianity* and *Evangelical Essentials*. It is too easy to make an argument from ignorance about the "contexts" of the quotations without reading them first. It is his "contexts" that I am bringing to light.

No one knew that he was an annihilationist until after he wrote *Evangelical Essentials*. There are those who insist he is not an annihilationist. Dr. J.I. Packer explains that Dr. Stott is indeed an annihilationist.

---

[3] John W. Yates III, "Pottering and Prayer" *Christianity Today* (April 2, 2001)

> Evangelicals in particular are increasingly uncertain about the ongoing existence of those who leave this world in unbelief. ... Recently however persons who may fairly be called accredited evangelicals of the main stream have written in favor of extinction, which they call either annihilationism or conditional immortality. ... These writers include ... John Stott, one of the best known and <u>most admired</u> evangelical leaders anywhere in the world, in *Essentials*, 1988.[4]

I believe that, if asked, he would confirm that everything he has written is affected by his annihilationism. "Beware of false prophets, which come to you in sheep's clothing, but inwardly they are ravening wolves" (Matthew 7:15). Evangelicals fear Dr. Stott. "And fear not them which kill the body, but are not able to kill the soul: but rather fear him which is able to destroy both soul and body in hell" (Matthew 10:28). They admire him. "These are murmurers, complainers, walking after their own lusts; and their mouth speaketh great swelling words, having men's persons in admiration because of advantage" (Jude 1:16).

Yet, Dr. Packer says my burden is "distasteful." He gives a positive review of "Evangelical Annihilationism," even though he disagrees with it.

> It is distasteful to argue in print against honored fellow-evangelicals, some of whom are good friends and others of whom (I mention Atkinson, Wenham, and Hughes particularly) are now with Christ, so I stop right here. ... When John Stott argues that "the ultimate annihilation of the wicked should at least be accepted as a legitimate, biblically founded alternative to their eternal conscious torment," he asks too much,

---

[4] Alister McGrath, The J.I. Packer Collection, "The Problem of Eternal Punishiment,", (InterVarsity Press, Downers Grove, 1999), 220-222

for the biblical foundations of this view prove on inspection, as we have seen, to be inadequate. But it would be wrong for differences of opinion on this matter to lead to breaches of fellowship, though it would be a very happy thing for the Christian world if the differences could be resolved.[5]

What could be a more fundamental contradiction than a gospel without hell? What kind of atonement would be for no hell? "If in this life only we have hope in Christ, we are of all men most miserable" (1 Corinthians 15:19). Could such an atonement for annihilation quantitatively save from the true, infinite hell? It is not distasteful to save souls from fire. "And others save with fear, pulling them out of the fire; hating even the garment spotted by the flesh" (Jude 1:23).

I have been very naïve about Dr. Stott's fame. The only person in my "Acknowledgments" (there were others I am grateful for) who knew I was not crazy was my psychiatrist. Dr. Gary L. Almy wrote the book description on the back. But an American Christian Writers editor took my money only to mock me and to tell me to throw this book away, even accusing me of "blasphemy" (against Dr. Stott). Other "pastors, teachers and friends" who I contacted responded with threats. Dr. Michael Horton of Westminster Seminary in California retorted that I was "straining gnats" (which would be the wrath of God?) and was in danger of "swallowing a camel" (which would be something more dangerous than the wrath of God?). They taught me what original sin is, and they don't know it themselves. Once they learned my topic, they refused to be sociable. The modern Reformation is unlearned and unstable unto their own destruction.

---

[5] J.I. Packer, "Evangelical annihilationism In Review,", *Reformation & Revival* magazine, Volume 6, Number 2 - Spring 1997

"And account that the longsuffering of our Lord
is salvation; even as our beloved brother Paul
also according to the wisdom given unto him
hath written unto you; As also in all his epistles,
speaking in them of these things; in which are
some things hard to be understood, which they
that are unlearned and unstable wrest, as they do
also the other scriptures, unto their own
destruction" (2 Peter 3:15-16).

Annihilationists do not believe in heaven or hell or their
need for an eternal sacrifice on their behalf. They preach peace
and no evil to the modern Reformation.

"Thus saith the LORD of hosts, Hearken not
unto the words of the prophets that prophesy
unto you: they make you vain: they speak a vision
of their own heart, and not out of the mouth of
the LORD. They say still unto them that despise
me, The LORD hath said, Ye shall have peace;
and they say unto every one that walketh after
the imagination of his own heart, No evil shall
come upon you. ... Therefore, behold, I, even I,
will utterly forget you, and I will forsake you, and
the city that I gave you and your fathers, and cast
you out of my presence: And I will bring an
everlasting reproach upon you, and a perpetual
shame, which shall not be forgotten" (Jeremiah
23:16, 17, 39, 40).

The prophets of peace and no evil make my pastors,
teachers and friends vain. Believing supporters of evangelical
annihilationists must escape from the everlasting reproach unto
everlasting righteousness because they listen to them.

God will require Dr. Stott's blood at my hands if I do
not warn him about sin. "When I say unto the wicked, Thou
shalt surely die; and thou givest him not warning, nor speakest to
warn the wicked from his wicked way, to save his life; the same

wicked man shall die in his iniquity; but his blood will I require at thine hand" (Ezekiel 3:18). Believing friends of annihilationists need to be warned about sin like righteous men. "Again, When a righteous man doth turn from his righteousness, and commit iniquity, and I lay a stumblingblock before him, he shall die: because thou hast not given him warning, he shall die in his sin, and his righteousness which he hath done shall not be remembered; but his blood will I require at thine hand" (Ezekiel 3:20). But I don't want anyone's blood at my hands on the day of judgment.

The "context" of the heretical quotes you are about to read is as systematic as true doctrine. "He that speaketh truth sheweth forth righteousness: but a false witness deceit" (Proverbs 12:17). If Dr. Stott writes existential contradictions, then that is another reason why he needs to be saved. I learned these doctrines and heresies by holding up his books in light of the Reformation. By negative example is the only way to learn the truth. I could not "leave Dr. Stott out of it" once I found the self-justifying existentialism in his works. It is bombastic that an annihilationist should author a book about the Cross of Christ. But, for all his humility, Dr. Stott is the consummate existentialist communicator. It is not my fault that no one else presumed or saw his denials of faith in his books.

The gates of annihilationism shall not prevail. "And I say also unto thee, That thou art Peter, and upon this rock I will build my church; and the gates of hell shall not prevail against it" (Matthew 16:18). Jesus will prevail. "To open their eyes, and to turn them from darkness to light, and from the power of Satan unto God, that they may receive forgiveness of sins, and inheritance among them which are sanctified by faith that is in me" (Acts 26:18). That being said, I have just about lassoed the moon for one Linda Piepenbrink.

II. INTRODUCTION TO ETERNAL THEOLOGY

A) Eternal Scripture and God. Before we look at eternal sin, let us first look at Scripture and God. Annihilationism proposes that there are finite scriptures about hell, but there are none. "For ever, O LORD, thy word is settled in heaven" (Psalms 119:89). Since the entire Bible is eternal, all finite doctrines are extra-biblical. "But the word of the Lord endureth for ever. And this is the word which by the gospel is preached unto you" (1 Peter 1:25). Finite ideas were not illuminated by God. Scriptures about hell are the tip of the iceberg of Dr. Stott's finite interpretations of all Scripture.

God's name is everlasting. "That led them by the right hand of Moses with his glorious arm, dividing the water before them, to make himself an everlasting name?" (Isaiah 63:12). And Jesus' name is everlasting. "For unto us a child is born, unto us a son is given: and the government shall be upon his shoulder: and his name shall be called Wonderful, Counsellor, The mighty God, The everlasting Father, The Prince of Peace" (Isaiah 9:6). To utter infinite God's name in the name of annihilationism is to take it in vain. "Thou shalt not take the name of the LORD thy God in vain; for the LORD will not hold him guiltless that taketh his name in vain" (Exodus 20:7).

"The LORD" means "The Self-Existent" or "The Eternal" (in the Strong's Hebrew Dictionary).

> H3068. Y@hovah
> hwhy Y@hovah yeh-ho-vaw'
> from 1961; (the) <u>self-Existent or Eternal</u>;
> Jehovah, Jewish national name of God:--Jehovah,
> the Lord. Compare 3050, 3069.

Existence is eternity also for man. "He has made everything beautiful in its time. He has also set <u>eternity in the hearts</u> of men; yet they cannot fathom what God has done from beginning to end" (Ecclesiastes 3:11, NIV). If we deny eternity, we deny existence, which is unpleasing to God. "But without faith it is impossible to please him: for he that cometh to God must believe that he is, and that he is a rewarder of them that diligently seek him" (Hebrews 11:6). That is why this book ends with Dr. Stott denying the name and existence of Christ.

B) Heaven and Conversion. Now let's look at why sin is eternal. Heaven is eternal. Ray Comfort explained in his book, aptly titled *Hell's Best Kept Secret*, that the belief in eternal heaven is essential for conversion.

> He now has light that his sin is primarily vertical: that he has "sinned against heaven" (Luke 15:21). That he has violated God's law and that he has angered God and the wrath of God abides upon Him (John 3:36). He can now see that he is "weighed in the balance" of eternal justice and "found wanting" (Daniel 5:27). He now understands the need for a sacrifice. "Christ redeemed from the curse of the law being made a curse for us" (Galatians 3:13). "God commended His love toward us in that while we were yet sinners Christ died for us" (Romans 5:8). We broke the law; he paid the fine. It's as simple as that.[6]

If our heaven is eternal, so will be our hell. This is not a post-mortem concern for would-be converts. Jonah's cry from the belly of the whale-hell was his conversion. "And [he] said, I cried by reason of mine affliction unto the LORD, and he heard me; out of the belly of hell cried I, and thou heardest my voice" (Jonah 2:2). King David experienced the same conversion. "The sorrows of death compassed me, and the pains of hell gat hold upon me: I found trouble and sorrow. Then called I upon the name of the LORD; O LORD, I beseech thee, deliver my soul" (Psalms 116:3-4). Jonah and King David had the same sense of

---

[6] Ray Comfort, www.LivingWaters.com, Living Waters Publications,. Bellflower, CA

the hell of original sin as all converts have had, and they cried out to Jesus. "That if thou shalt confess with thy mouth the Lord Jesus, and shalt believe in thine heart that God hath raised him from the dead, thou shalt be saved" (Romans 10:9). But conversion depends upon the awareness in this life of eternal hell!

C) The Infinite God's Revelation. All great revivals, including Luther, John Calvin and Jonathan Edwards, were based upon the preaching of eternal conscious torment. Martin Luther explained that his famous Ninety-five Theses were about infinite justice. He showed that, if we reason finitely, we are trying to justify ourselves, which never saves. Everything is eternal from God's perspective. This infinite God's revelation is the "context" of all Evangelical Orthodoxy. It is also the "context" of all the proof-texts against Dr. Stott. And self-justifying finite reason is the "context" of all reprobation. This is Dr. Stott's "context."

> [Finite] Reason is naturally self-justifying, Luther says ... the law comes to condemn, as the preparation for the gospel, telling the person what his self-justifying reason would not: that he is a sinner. ... The person [is] thus humbled, [3 Justification] given the gift of faith in Christ, will then trust God even when God tells him that the penalty for sin is death -- [1 Original Sin] be that the death of the sinner or [2 Atonement] the death of the Substitute. ... it would be utterly insane for the reason of finite creatures to ignore the limits prescribed by the infinite God's revelation.[7]

Luther's Ninety-five Theses sang an example of the infinite God's revelation. They were about how finite

---

[7] Benjamin E. Sasse "Neither Reason Nor Free-Will Points To Him," *Modern Reformation*, (Nov./Dec. 1998)

indulgences do not save from eternal conscious torment. They were about their "inefficacy," because purgatory was self-justifying reason, not unlike annihilationism. Purgatory and indulgences are finite.

1. Our Lord and Master Jesus Christ, when He said *Poenitentiam agite*, willed that the whole life of believers should be [infinite] repentance.
16. Hell [eternal conscious torment], purgatory [or annihilation], and heaven seem to differ as do despair, almost-despair, and the assurance of safety.
21. Therefore those preachers of indulgences are in error, who say that by the pope's indulgences a man is freed from every penalty, and [eternally] saved.
68. Yet they are in truth the very smallest [slight] graces compared with the [eternal] grace of God and the piety of the Cross.
92. Away, then, with all those prophets who say to the people of Christ, "Peace, peace," and there is no peace! [8]

In the first thesis, Luther (according to the infinite God's revelation) implies that we need infinite repentance. His arguments for confessing original sin (the infinite death of the sinner) against almost-despair purgatory are in 16 and 92. He shows us false finite justification in 21. Finite indulgences are the smallest graces but not eternal. "For they have healed [saved] the hurt [eternal conscious torment] of the daughter of my people slightly, saying, Peace, peace; when there is no peace" (Jeremiah 8:11). The sense of full, immortal "despair" frightens out of purgatory unto the atonement in 68. Both annihilation and purgatory are the same almost-despair. Roman Catholics and

---

[8] Martin Luther, *Ninety-five Theses* (Disputation of Doctor Martin Luther on the Power and Efficacy of Indulgences) (1517)

everyone who creatively violates original sin (also Nirvana) are still under its eternal condemnation.

D) Imputation. The infinite God's revelation and the Ninety-five Theses are further delineated as Imputation.

> [1] Original Sin, [2] Atonement, [3] Justification: [...]The act of imputation is precisely the same in each case. [1] It is not meant that Adam's [eternal] sin was personally the sin of his descendants, but that it was set to their account, so that they share its guilt and [eternal] penalty. [2] It is not meant that Christ shares personally in the sins of men, but that the guilt of his people's [eternal] sin was set to his account, so that He bore its [eternal] penalty. [3] It is not meant that Christ's people are made personally holy or inwardly righteous by the imputation of His [eternal] righteousness to them, but that His righteousness is set to their account, so that they are entitled to all the rewards of that perfect [eternal] righteousness.[9]

An imputation is an external judgment that may or may not reflect one's own personal deeds. It is a declaration of how a person will be treated. Original sin came from Adam, but it applies equally to all mankind, no matter who you are. Hence, I am not comparing Dr. Stott to myself. All three (the first two are the same wrath) imputations are forever. "I know that whatsoever God doeth, it shall be for ever: nothing can be put to it, nor any thing taken from it: and God doeth it, that men should fear before him" (Ecclesiastes 3:14). Therefore, God judges original sin, atonement and justification infinitely and absolutely. God's ways are equal. "A just weight and balance are the LORD'S: all the weights of the bag are his work" (Proverbs

---

[9] Caspar Wistar Hodge, *The International Standard Bible Encyclopedia*, "Imputation," (1915)

16:11). Because imputation is about infinite math, it is impossible for annihilationists to affirm infinite imputation. Imputation is the key to all Scripture.

E) Declaration of Faith. Here is the infinite God's revelation, and the exact same three imputations flushed out even further by the Armitage Baptist Church's Southern Baptist Declaration of Faith. They are all eternal.

We believe that man, being created by a direct act of God (Gen. 2:7, John 1:1-3), was a righteous, free, moral being (Eccl. 7:29, Gen. 1:27, Eph. 4:24); that he sinned (Gen. 3:6-7, Rom. 5:18) and thereby incurred the penalty of <u>physical and spiritual death</u> (Gen. 2:17, Rom. 6:23, <u>Rev. 20:14-15),</u> not only for himself but also for the entire human race, with the result that we are all sinful by nature (Rom. 3:10, Rom. 5:12-19, Psa. 51:5).
We believe that Jesus Christ, by His <u>substitutionary death</u> on the cross (1 Peter 2:24, 2 Cor. 5:21), secured salvation for all those who will receive Him as their only Savior (Rom. 10:13, John 1:12); that these, who are regenerated by the Holy Spirit (John 3:6, Titus 3:5), will never perish (John 10:27-30, Rom. 8:35-39); and that it is impossible for anyone to be saved except by Jesus Christ (Acts 4:12, 1 Tim. 2:5).
We believe in the ultimate triumph of Jesus Christ, <u>His</u> church and <u>righteousness</u> at His glorious appearing (2 Thess. 1:8-10, Rev. 19:11-16), in the resurrection of the dead (John 5:24-30, 1 Cor. 15:12-19, Rev. 20:12-15), in the <u>eternal blessedness of the saved</u> (John 14:1-3, Rev. 22:1-5) and in the <u>eternal conscious suffering of the</u>

> unsaved (Mark 9:42-48, Luke 16:19-31, Rev. 21:8).[10]

These are the same three sub-points in the teachings on the infinite God's revelation and imputation above. This Baptist confession invokes Revelation for original sin (see the first point). "And death and hell were cast into the lake of fire. This is the second death. And whosoever was not found written in the book of life was cast into the lake of fire" (Revelation 20:14-15). Salvation from original sin at the beginning of the Bible is based upon the fear of it in this life. "Again, he limiteth a certain day, saying in David, To day, after so long a time; as it is said, To day if ye will hear his voice, harden not your hearts" (Hebrews 4:7). Then we escape to the second stage where Jesus was our Substitute for stage one, our "physical and spiritual death" (eternal conscious torment). What is spiritual is eternal. Spirituality is infinite. But, by definition, annihilationists deny stages one and two. The last stage is His "righteousness at His glorious appearing," which is the fulfillment of justification by faith alone according to the earlier Substitution. Annihilationists cannot affirm the eternal blessedness of the saved without also affirming His sinless substitutionary death for their own physical and spiritual death.

We are embarking on a tour of the infinite God's revelation versus Dr. Stott's finite existentialism. First, we will see how he denies the Law, original sin, punishment and repentance. Second, we will see him deny how Christ took our punishment upon Himself as our Substitute and his invalid alternatives to the atonement. Third, we will see how he denies the benefit of eternal pardon and justification and teaches legalism. Then we will see how his legalism is driven by the denial of the resurrection, unregenerate flesh and heathen power lust, even after the teachings of Fredrick Nietzsche. Finally, we shall witness his denial of the existence and name of Jesus Christ. It is my goal to bring as many readers, including Dr. Stott, to the eternal gospel as God has chosen. But I don't want

---

[10] Armitage Baptist Church, Chicago, Declaration of Faith.

any doubt that I am writing that Dr. Stott denies essential beliefs and is unsaved for it. May God bless your reading of this book. There are 38 Dr. Stott quotations altogether.

III. ETERNAL SIN AGAINST HEAVEN

A) Eternal Life. Ray Comfort explained in *Hell's Best Kept Secret* that, if we believe in eternal heaven, we will have eternal repentance. "For God so loved the world, that he gave his only begotten Son, that whosoever believeth in him should not perish, but have everlasting life" (John 3:16). The foundation of repentance is hope. "The Lord is not slack concerning his promise [also promises], as some men count slackness; but is longsuffering to us-ward, not willing that any should perish, but that all should come to repentance" (2 Peter 3:9). John Calvin agrees that faith works repentance.

> For when our Lord and John begin their preaching thus "Repent, for the kingdom of heaven is at hand" (Matthew 3:2), do they not deduce repentance as a consequence of the offer of grace and promise of salvation? The force of the words, therefore, is the same as if it were said, "As the kingdom of heaven is at hand, for that reason repent ..." Then, according to the passage in the Psalms, "There is forgiveness with thee, that thou mayest be feared" (Psalm 130:4),.no man will ever reverence God who does not trust that God is propitious to him, no man will ever willingly set himself to observe the Law who is not persuaded that his services are pleasing to God.[11]

---

[11] John Calvin, *Institutes of The Christian Religion*, Henry Beveridge (1581) 3.3.2.

Our heaven must be eternal for us to be saved from
earth and hell. Does Dr. Stott believe in eternal life? Dr. Stott
asserts a finite heaven.

> 1. Finite heaven.
> [...] the new heaven and new earth, and the New
> Jerusalem, in which there will be no tears, death,
> pain or night, as God establishes his perfect
> rule.[12]

He says "there will be no tears, death, pain or night," but
the verse he is citing says "reign for ever and ever." "And there
shall be no night there; and they need no candle, neither light of
the sun; for the Lord God giveth them light: and they shall reign
for ever and ever" (Revelation 22:5). It does not say "perfect
reign." God's Law quantitatively exceeds qualitative perfection.
"I have seen an end of all perfection: but thy commandment is
exceeding broad" (Psalms 119:96). It says that believers will rule,
but he says that it is God's rule. Dr. Stott does not have the faith
in eternal heaven to believe in eternal sin or hell, and he does
not.

B) The Divine Moral *A Priori*. It makes sense that
immortal hell would be guaranteed for disobedience in the
immortal Garden of Eden. "But of the tree of the knowledge of
good and evil, thou shalt not eat of it: for in the day that thou
eatest thereof thou shalt surely die" (Genesis 2:17). But as he
rejected eternal heaven, Dr. Stott also rejected the command to
Adam to not eat of the tree (and also the atonement for it).

> "For Christ also hath once suffered for sins, the
> [morally] just for the [morally] unjust, that he
> might bring us to God, being put to death in the
> flesh, but quickened by the Spirit" (1 Peter 3:18).

---

[12] John Stott, *The Cross of Christ*, (Downers Grove: IVP, 1986), 250

2. No Divine moral *a priori.*
It is perilous to begin with any *a priori*, even with a God-given sense of moral justice which then shapes our understanding of the cross.[13]

In other words, he denies the moral justice of both the commandment and the atonement, both of which we see clearly in 1 Peter 3:18. He attacks moral justice because it is eternal. "Of the doctrine of baptisms, and of laying on of hands, and of resurrection of the dead, and of eternal judgment" (Hebrews 6:2). Generally, the term "moral *a priories*" means all moral standards of any kind. This is not from his biographies.

C) Original Sin. Adam's sin was immortal since it occurred in the immortal Garden of Eden. Here is imputation explained once again.

> Adam's sin was imputed to the entire human race. We were made guilty before God not by a process of sin being infused into us, but by a declaration of our solidarity with Adam as our representative head. In exactly the same way, Paul says, Christ's righteousness is imputed to all believers by virtue of their union with him. The imputation of righteousness is just as forensic or legal as the imputation of sin: The judgment followed one sin and brought condemnation, but the gift followed many trespasses and brought justification. Are our opponents really willing to argue that condemnation is a moral process? Jesus said that he who does not believe stands condemned already, just as the one who believes has passed from death unto life.[14]

---

[13] Stott, *The Cross of Christ,* 104
[14] Dr. Michael Horton, "Justification, Vital Now & Always," *Modern Reformation* (March/April 1994)

Adam was our *a priori* "representative head" sinner. "Therefore, as through one man sin entered into the world, and death through sin; and so death passed unto all men, for that all sinned" (Romans 5:12). But Dr. Horton does not suspect that Dr. Stott would violate original sin. He is correct that imputation is not a self-justifying moral process. However, he does not seem to understand that the problem is that a moral process is *finite* justice. Original sin is eternal judgment, and annihilation is a moral process of self-justification. Nevertheless, he correctly points us back to a confession of original sin as the doorway to our justification by faith.

Here is original sin: "...he [Adam] sinned (Genesis 3:6-7; Romans 5:18) and thereby incurred the penalty of physical and spiritual death (Genesis 2:17; Romans 6:23; Revelation 20:14-15), not only for himself but also for the entire human race ..."[15] Dr. Stott replaces it with a finite, self-justifying, moral process, which Dr. Horton warned us about, limited to individuals east of Eden.

3. No original sin.
Sinners therefore incur the penalty of their law-breaking.[16]

He omits and replaces "that (Adam) sinned -- not only for himself but also for the entire human race" with finite individuals after the fall. He changes it from past tense to future progressive tense, a moral process that does not condemn, not a forensic moral *a priori*. Hence, "law-breaking" might be sociological alcoholism or psychological guilt, but not sin in the immortal Garden against heaven and God. Of course, Dr. Stott would say that the "penalty" is not eternal torment that comes from Adam. We already know that Dr. Stott rejects the *a priori* divine moral commandment to not eat of the tree. Even individual sins are eternal. "For whosoever shall keep the whole law, and yet offend in one point, he is guilty of all" (James 2:10).

---

[15] Armitge Baptist Church, Chicago, Declaration of Faith
[16] Stott, *The Cross of Christ*, 114.

D) Eternal Sin. Here are scriptures about eternal sin.

"I will arise and go to my father, and will say unto him, Father, I have sinned against heaven, and before thee" (Luke 15:18).

"And beside all this, between us and you there is a great gulf fixed: so that they which would pass from hence to you cannot; neither can they pass to us, that would come from thence" (Luke 16:26).

"But your iniquities have separated between you and your God, and your sins have hid his face from you, that he will not hear" (Isaiah 59:2).

"What thing shall I take to witness for thee? what thing shall I liken to thee, O daughter of Jerusalem? what shall I equal to thee, that I may comfort thee, O virgin daughter of Zion? for thy breach is great like the sea: who can heal thee?" (Lamentations 2:13).

The law requires continual obedience. "For as many as are of the works of the law are under the curse: for it is written, Cursed is every one that continueth not in all things which are written in the book of the law to do them" (Galatians 3:10). Because the law is "continual," we must acknowledge that sin is "exceeding." "Was then that which is good made death unto me? God forbid. But sin, that it might appear sin, working death in me by that which is good; that sin by the commandment might become exceeding sinful" (Romans 7:13). All sin is eternal. "Is not thy wickedness great? and thine iniquities infinite?" (Job 22:5).

But Dr. Stott's law is not continuous, and his sin is not exceeding. In this quote, Dr. Stott launches a finite diatribe against God's eternal gulf.

5. No eternal sin.
Fundamental to it [annihilationism] is the belief that God will judge people "according to what they [have] done" (e.g. Revelation 20:12), This principal had been applied in the Jewish law courts ... in which penalties were limited to an exact retribution, "life for life, eye for eye, tooth for tooth, hand for hand, foot for foot" (e.g. Exodus 21:23-25). Would there not, then, be a serious disproportion between sins consciously committed in time and torment consciously experienced throughout eternity?[17]

He finitely "limited" the Holy Judge. "Yea, they turned back and tempted God, and limited the Holy One of Israel" (Psalms 78:41). But the holy God is eternal, and Dr. Stott is not. The term "reprobate" means "void of judgment," which we have seen much of. Eternal hell is worse than losing body parts. "Wherefore if thy hand or thy foot offend thee, cut them off, and cast them from thee: it is better for thee to enter into life halt or maimed, rather than having two hands or two feet to be cast into everlasting fire" (Matthew 18:8). Therefore we have established theory that Dr. Stott's denial of hell is evidence of the denial of sin.

Annihilationism mathematically destroys heaven since there is only one common judgment: Would there not, then, also be a serious disproportion between good deeds consciously committed in time and grace consciously experienced throughout eternity? The doctrine of imputation is symmetrical, absolute and perpetual. "And these shall go away into everlasting punishment: but the righteous into life eternal" (Matthew 25:46). But the modern Reformation has succumbed to the denial of two distinct imputations (see Dr. Horton's explanation of original sin and justification). Dr. Stott only has one singular destination—not a separate heaven and hell. His moral process

---

[17] John Stott and Dale Edwards, *Evangelical Essentials*, (Downers Grove: IVP, 1989), 318

of finite justice is singular, chaotic and deteriorating, which describes his entire afterlife. The Reformation has also succumbed to finite sin. But Dr. Stott is trying to conquer exceeding sin by denying it.

E) Sin Nature. Dr. Stott rejects the sin nature.

Moral anemia is the sin nature. "When Jesus heard it, he saith unto them, They that are whole have no need of the physician, but they that are sick: I came not to call the [hypocritically] righteous, but sinners to repentance" (Mark 2:17). We must repent for it. "And the publican, standing afar off, would not lift up so much as his eyes unto heaven, but smote upon his breast, saying, God be merciful to me a sinner" (Luke 18:13). I, Jim Cronfel, am a moral anemic. "There is none that understandeth, there is none that seeketh after God" (Romans 3:11). We cannot conquer it by denial. "Can the Ethiopian change his skin, or the leopard his spots? then may ye also do good, that are accustomed to do evil" (Jeremiah 13:23). It is in our bodies. "For I know that in me (that is, in my flesh,) dwelleth no good thing: for to will is present with me; but how to perform that which is good I find not" (Romans 7:18). We were born into it. "Behold, I was shapen in iniquity; and in sin did my mother conceive me" (Psalms 51:5). It is unsolvable. "The heart is deceitful above all things, and desperately wicked: who can know it?" (Jeremiah 17:9).

4. Steers away sinners.
If you suffer from moral anaemia, take my advice and steer clear of Christianity.[18]

He does not believe in sin or sinners, and he compares himself to others. Jesus tells us to steer away from all those who deny it. "Having a form of godliness, but denying the power thereof: from such turn away" (2 Timothy 3:5).

---

[18] John Stott, *Basic Christianity* (Downers Grove: IVP, 1958), 119

F) The Law Of Punishment. To reject sin and sinners, Dr. Stott must do away with the eternal Law.

> 6. No fiery punishment or law-language.
> Nevertheless, we need to be alert to the dangers of law-language. … For example, "if you put your hand in the fire it will be burnt, and if you break the Ten Commandments you will be punished"[19]

Do you see how he is negating the law? "Law-breaking" is not punished according to "law-language." This is another reprobated "voiding of judgment." And it is an argument against fire and brimstone. No one but me cares enough to tell him that God will punish him if he does not repent. "What wilt thou say when he shall punish thee? for thou hast taught them to be captains, and as chief over thee: shall not sorrows take thee, as a woman in travail?" (Jeremiah 13:21). He has rejected his own conversion with the Law. "The law of the LORD is perfect, converting the soul: the testimony of the LORD is sure, making wise the simple" (Psalms 19:7).

To save us from it, Jesus fulfilled (obeyed) the Law. "Think not that I am come to destroy the law, or the prophets: I am not come to destroy, but to fulfill" (Matthew 5:17). But, to save himself from it, Dr. Stott destroys the Law. "It is time for thee, LORD, to work: for they have made void thy law" (Psalms 119:126). He never feared the schoolmaster unto Christ. "Wherefore the law was our schoolmaster to bring us unto Christ, that we might be justified by faith" (Galatians 3:24). There can be no justification by faith without the Law.

G) Spiritual Desperation. John Calvin teaches fiery law language.

> Let Him, I say, sit in judgment on the actions of men, and who will feel secure in sisting himself

---

[19] Stott, *The Cross of Christ*, 116

before his throne? "Who among us," says the prophets "shall dwell with the devouring fire? who among us shall dwell with everlasting burnings? He that walketh righteously, and speaketh uprightly," &c. (Isaiah 33:14, 15). Let whoso will come forth. Nay, the answer shows that no man can. For, on the other hand, we hear the dreadful voice: "If thou, Lord, shouldst mark our iniquities, O Lord, who shall stand?" (Psalms 130:3). All must immediately perish, as Job declares, "Shall mortal man be more just than God? shall a man be more pure than his Maker? Behold, he put no trust in his servants; and his angels he charged with folly: How much less in them that dwell in houses of clay, whose foundation is in the dust, which are crushed before the moth? They are destroyed from morning to evening" (Job 4:17-20). [20]

But, since he did away with the Law, Dr. Stott feels secure sisting, mocking God's judgment throne.

7. Hell is rejected not feared.

Well, emotionally, I find the concept [of eternal conscious torment] intolerable and do not understand how people can live with it without either cauterizing their feelings or cracking under the strain. ... [21]

I have cauterized feelings and have cracked under the strain (see the back matter). "The fear of the LORD is the beginning of wisdom: and the knowledge of the holy is understanding" (Proverbs 9:10). He needs to be delivered. "The angel of the LORD encampeth round about them that fear him,

---

[20] Calvin, *Institutes*, 3.12.1

[21] Stott, *Evangelical Essentials*, 314

and delivereth them" (Psalm 34:7). He needs to be driven to the Cross. "The LORD reigneth; let the people tremble: he sitteth between the cherubims; let the earth be moved" (Psalms 99:1). He is in danger for rejecting fiery judgment. "I tell you, Nay: but, except ye repent, ye shall all likewise perish" (Luke 13:3). *Dr. Stott tolerates it more than believers, or else he would have escaped from it. If he knew how horrible it was, he would not mock God.*

H) Hell Comes after Death. I think that a staunch annihilationist would agree that everything he has written is affected by his annihilationism. Here he psychologically "symbolizes" the burning "lake of fire" into a present-tense, "ghastly thirst of the soul."

> 8. Hell is only in this world.
> ... if in this world we deliberately reject Jesus Christ ... It is also called in the Bible "the second death" and "the lake of fire," terms which describe symbolically the forfeiture of eternal life and the ghastly thirst of the soul. ...
>
> It is this that accounts for the restlessness of men and women today ... This situation is tragic beyond words. Man is missing the destiny for which God made him. [22]

I underlined the present tense language so you can see how his "second death" only "accounts for the restlessness of men and women today." Unbelievers say that hell is only in this life. But the second death is after the first death. "And death and hell were cast into the lake of fire. This is the second death" (Revelation 20:14). He says that "this situation is tragic beyond words." But hell is far beyond tragic words. "The sting of death is sin; and the strength of sin is the law" (1 Corinthians 15:56). He is "almost-desperate," as in Luther's argument against purgatory.

---

[22] Stott, *Basic Christianity*, 73-75

He only has the sorrow of this world. "For godly sorrow worketh repentance to salvation not to be repented of: but the sorrow of the world worketh death" (2 Corinthians 7:10). He is lukewarm. "So then because thou art lukewarm, and neither cold nor hot, I will spue thee out of my mouth" (Revelation 3:16). He still hopes in himself. "Thou art wearied in the greatness of thy way; yet saidst thou not, There is no hope: thou hast found the life of thine hand; therefore thou wast not grieved" (Isaiah 57:10).

I) Darwinism and Unconversion. If you follow the annihilationism debate, then you know that they deny the immortality of the soul so it can be annihilated. John Calvin defended the immortality of the soul against soulless evolution. This is a test of conversion.

> How could motion devoid of essence penetrate to the judgement-seat of God, and under a <u>sense of guilt</u> strike itself with terror? The body cannot be affected by any fear of spiritual punishment. This is competent only to the soul, which must therefore be endued with essence. Then the mere knowledge of a God sufficiently proves that souls which rise higher than the world must be immortal, it being impossible that any evanescent vigour could reach the very fountain of life. In fine, while the many noble faculties with which the human mind is endued proclaim that something divine is engraven on it, there are so many evidences of an immortal essence. For such <u>sense as the lower animals possess</u> goes not beyond the body, or at least not beyond the objects actually presented to it. [23]

---

[23] Calvin, *Institutes*, 1.15.2

9. Animal soullessness for Christ and man.

Christ died our death, when he died for our sins … the sense of anomaly that man should have become "like the beasts that perish [*are annihilated*]," since "the same fate awaits them both."[24]

Dr. Stott's unconverted, soulless, theistic evolution revolves around the word "perish." Animals are annihilated, and they don't need to repent because they do not suffer from moral anemia nor are they punished according to law language. We would not be subject to eternal conscious torment – not even on the Cross – if mankind and Christ were soulless animals that "perished." Lower animals do not posses awareness. "Who teacheth us more than the beasts of the earth, and maketh us wiser than the fowls of heaven?" (Job 35:11). Evolution is another rejection of creation like Dr. Stott's denial of God's commandment to Adam. He does not have an infinite God-shaped hole in his soul (heart). "Speaking lies in hypocrisy; having their conscience seared with a hot iron" (1 Timothy 4:2).

Converts' souls are eternal. "He has also set eternity in the hearts of men; yet they cannot fathom what God has done from beginning to end" (Ecclesiastes 3:11, NIV). Conversion concerns the heart's awareness of hell. "Hell and destruction are before the LORD: how much more then the hearts of the children of men?" (Proverbs 15:11). Human beasts are reprobates. "But these, as natural brute beasts, made to be taken and destroyed, speak evil of the things that they understand not; and shall utterly perish in their own corruption" (2 Peter 2:12).

His "another Christ" literally has no soul or awareness to allow for its annihilation on the Cross. Jesus had a soul. "And saith unto them, My soul is exceeding sorrowful unto death: tarry ye here, and watch" (Mark 14:34). His soulless Christ is the antichrist beast. "And the devil that deceived them was cast into the lake of fire and brimstone, where the beast and the false prophet are, and

---

[24] Stott, *The Cross of Christ*, 64-65

shall be tormented day and night for ever and ever" (Revelation 20:10). But the atonement was not about the soulless beasts.

> "Neither by the blood of goats and calves, but by his own blood he entered in once into the holy place, having obtained <u>eternal redemption</u> for us. For if the blood of bulls and of goats, and the ashes of an heifer sprinkling the unclean, sanctifieth to the purifying of the flesh: How much more shall the blood of Christ, who through the <u>eternal Spirit</u> offered himself without spot to God, purge your conscience from dead works to serve the living God? And for this cause he is the mediator of the new testament, that by means of death, for the redemption of the transgressions that were under the first testament, they which are called might receive the promise of <u>eternal inheritance</u>" (Hebrews 9:12-15).

Are there any scriptures that say that Jesus *eternally* redeemed us? Above, we see that the Old Testament, Judaic, legalistic, animal sacrifice system involved finite goat and calf annihilations. But our atonement was "eternal redemption" "through the eternal Spirit" for our "eternal inheritance" through the eternal Christ. But Dr. Stott reduces Christ back down into a soulless goat or calf for annihilation. Therefore, annihilationism is a continuation or culmination of basic Old Testament, ritualistic Judaism on Golgotha.

Dr. Stott does not believe in heaven, the Law, divine moral justice, exceeding sin, punishment, the sin nature, human souls or Christ's soul, repentance or hell.

IV. VICARIOUS, SUBSTITUTIONARY, SACRIFICIAL, ETERNAL CONSCIOUS TORMENT; WHY GOD BECAME MAN

A) Evangelical Penal Substitution Defined. Jesus sinlessly lived and died for us. "Then said he, Lo, I come to do thy [eternal] will, O God. He taketh away the first, that he may establish the second. By the which will we are sanctified [and justified] through the [eternal] offering of the [eternal] body of Jesus Christ once for all" (Hebrews 10:9-10). It is not meant that Christ shares personally in the sins of men but that the guilt of His people's eternal sin was set to His account so that He bore its eternal penalty.

> "For Christ also hath once suffered for sins, the just for the unjust, that he might bring us to God, being put to death in the flesh, but quickened by the Spirit" (1 Peter 3:18).

> "For God so loved the world, that he gave his only begotten Son, that whosoever believeth in him should not perish, but have everlasting life" (John 3:16).

> "For if, when we were enemies, we were reconciled to God by the death of his Son, much more, being reconciled, we shall be saved by his life" (Romans 5:10).

> "And that he might reconcile both unto God in one body by the cross, having slain the enmity thereby" (Ephesians 2:16).

He took our eternal place. "For he hath made him to be sin for us, who knew no sin; that we might be made the righteousness of God in him" (2 Corinthians 5:21). The Father sent the eternal Son instead of eternally condemning us. "For what the law could not do, in that it was weak through the flesh, God sending his own Son in the likeness of sinful flesh, and for sin, condemned sin in the flesh" (Romans 8:3). He was our eternal propitiation. "Whom God hath set forth to be a propitiation through faith in his blood, to declare his righteousness for the remission of sins that are past, through the forbearance of God" (Romans 3:25). He was eternally cursed. "Christ hath redeemed us from the curse of the law, being made a curse for us: for it is written, 'Cursed is every one that hangeth on a tree'" (Galatians 3:13). We are eternally reconciled with the holy God. "Jesus saith unto him, 'I am the way, the truth, and the life: no man cometh unto the Father, but by me'" (John 14:6).

St. Anselm of Canterbury (1033 – 1109) was a famous teacher of the above scriptures about the infinite God's revelation before Luther. Here is the infinite debt from Adam and the definition of penal substitution.

Anselm is also remembered for setting forth a major understanding of the atonement in his treatise *Why [the infinite] God Became Man*. Since [through Adam] humans incurred an infinite debt to God when they sinned, and since only [the righteous Omnipotent] God could pay this great debt, God became human in Jesus Christ to offer satisfaction for sinful humanity through His death on the cross. This understanding of the cross, later clarified by John Calvin, has remained an important part of the evangelical understanding of atonement. [25]
In summary, penal substitution is the death of Christ [righteously] bearing the punishment justly due sinners by the guilt of their sins being imputed to Him (set down to His account) in

---

[25] David S. Dockery *Holman Bible Handbook* "Anselm" Quickverse Essentials Bible Software www.findex.com

> such a way that He representatively bore their
> eternal punishment. [26]

Jesus, the infinite God-man, came between sinful man
up to God the Father. He sinlessly, substitutionally bore our
eternal punishment.

B) Substitution Denied. Yet, in the last chapter, Dr.
Stott said that eternal sin was "perilous" and "intolerable." And
he said that law language was "dangerous." The terms "crude"
and "legalistic" are more unbelieving conventions, only applied
to vicarious substitution (that another person would pay for
someone else's crime).

10. & 11. Penal Substitution is crude.

> It is worth noting that the "fire and brimstone"
> school of theology who revel in ideas such as
> that Christ was made a sacrifice to appease an
> angry God, or that the cross was a legal
> transaction in which an innocent victim was
> made to pay the penalty for the crimes of
> others ... came into Christian theology by way
> of the legalistic minds of the medieval
> churchmen; they are not biblical Christianity.
> ... It is doubtful if anybody has ever believed
> such a crude construction. [27]

> Such crude interpretations of the cross still
> emerge in some of our evangelical illustrations,
> as we describe Christ as coming to rescue us
> from the judgment of God, or when we portray
> him as the whipping-boy who is punished
> instead of the real culprit. [28]

> a repeat] It is perilous to begin with any *a priori*,

---

[26] Dr. Steve Sullivan at John Ankerberg's Theological Research Institute,
Theological Dictionary , "Substitution" www.ankerberg.com

[27] Stott, *The Cross of Christ*, 172-173
[28] Ibid., 150

> even with a God-given sense of moral justice which then shapes our understanding of the cross.[29]

If he believed that Jesus was eternally punished, he would not be an annihilationist. He rejects "fire and brimstone" against himself and also vicarious eternal justice against Christ. He lashes out at Anselm and Calvin as "legalistic medieval churchmen." This is yet more reprobated voiding of judgment. If he does not repent, he will burn for his disobedience to the gospel. "In flaming fire taking vengeance on them that know not God, and that obey not the Gospel of our Lord Jesus Christ" (2 Thessalonians 1:8). We already saw him reject divine moral justice to begin with. He is being consistent and predictable.

C) Punishment not Patripassianism. The reason why Dr. Stott denies the punishment on the Cross is because he denies the very existence of Christ because of His inherent liability to punishment in relation to the Father. See how he even twists the true gospel, "(that God punished Jesus for our sins)," into "the other formulation."

12. & 13. & 14. Patripassianism Asserted.

> As for the other formulation (that God punished Jesus for our sins) [his parenthesis] ... We must not, then, speak of God punishing Jesus or of Jesus persuading God for to do so is to set them over against each other as if they acted independently of each other ... We must never make Christ the object of God's punishment or God the object of Christ's persuasion, for both God and Christ were subjects not objects ... [30]
>
> There is no question now of the Father

---

[29] Stott, *The Cross of Christ*, 104
[30] Ibid., 151

> inflicting punishment on the Son or of the Son
> intervening on our behalf with the Father, for it
> is the Father himself who takes the initiative in
> his love, bears the penalty of sin himself, and so
> dies. [31]
>
> it is the Judge himself who in holy love
> assumed the role of the innocent victim, for in
> and through the person of his Son he himself
> bore the penalty which he himself inflicted." [32]

In the first quote, his father and son were both the same subject so that there was no punishment against the Son. In the second quote, he succinctly and existentially replaces the Son with the Father, even though he contradictorily invokes the name of the Son. He is not refuting heresies beyond our comprehension. Rather, his existentialism is beyond our comprehension. Instead of having the Father judge Christ the Substitute for our sins, his PERSON of a false father, "The Judge," came to earth to commit suicide, to kill and void judgment against sin itself instead of paying for sin. (Or is he saying that the DIVINITY of God died?) He teaches another Jesus that is the Father. "For if he that cometh preacheth another Jesus, whom we have not preached, or if ye receive another spirit, which ye have not received, or another Gospel, which ye have not accepted, ye might well bear with him" (2 Corinthians 11:4). Yet the modern Reformation bears with him.

The heresy that "the Father himself ... bears the penalty of sin himself, and so dies," is named "Patripassianism." Ancient Church Father Tertullain showed that Patripassianism is antichrist.

> You have him crying aloud at his passion, My
> God, my God, why hast thou forsaken me?
> (Matthew 27:46). Consequently either the Son
> was suffering [in His manhood], forsaken by the

---

[31] Ibid., 152
[32] Ibid, 159

Father, and the Father did not suffer, seeing he
had forsaken the Son [in His manhood]: or else,
if it was the Father who was suffering, to what
God was he crying aloud? ...

... Therefore let them beware, these antichrists
who deny the Father and the Son (1 John 2:22).
For they do deny the Father while they identify
him with the Son, and they deny the Son while
they identify him with the Father, granting them
things they are not and taking away things they
are. But *he who shall confess that Christ is the Son of
God* – not the Father – *God abideth in him and he in
God* (1 John 4:15). [33]

The true Jesus shed His blood up to our Father who
remained in heaven. "Who needeth not daily, as those high
priests, to offer up sacrifice, first for his own sins, and then for
the people's: for this he did once, when he offered up himself"
(Hebrews 7:27). But Dr. Stott's descended father cried out to
himself instead of Jesus crying up to the true Father. But there
was no one left up in his finite heaven to receive his false father's
sacrifice. Therefore, Dr. Stott's false father sacrificed himself
down to bloodthirsty men on earth, not up to his finite heaven.
It was voodoo, cannibal sin-offering, dripping upside-down unto
himself. He has inverted the atonement against moral justice. It
is a riddle wrapped in a mystery inside an enigma.

D) Eternal Sin-Bearing not Moral Display. Here we
see a worthless "moral display" cross, a good example or
influence of how we should atone for ourselves. Annihilationism
converts the atonement into a moral display.

> ... Abelard's ideas seemed to go beyond the

---

[33] Terttulian, *Against Praxeas,*. Canon Ernest Evans trans. (SPCK, 1948).
section 31

> bounds of historic Christian orthodoxy on several important points. He challenged Anselm's understanding of the atonement by claiming that the cross was primarily a moral display of divine love rather than a required [eternal] satisfaction for human sin. [34]
>
> The denial of endless punishment] blots out the attribute of retributive justice; transmutes sin into misfortune, instead of guilt; turns all suffering into chastisement; converts the atonement work of Christ into moral influence [display]; and makes it a debt due to man, instead of an unmerited boon from God. [35]

15. Moral display replaces eternal sin-bearing.
... God in Christ bore our sins and died our death because of his love and justice, we must not think of it as expressing eternal sin-bearing in the heart of God. What Scripture does give us warrant to say, however, is that God's eternal holy love, which was uniquely exhibited in the sacrifice on the cross, continues to suffer with us in every situation in which it is called forth. [36]

Eternal sin-bearing simply means that He bore our eternal conscious torment. But Dr. Stott knew what to attack after attacking eternal sin: ETERNAL SIN-BEARING. Once again we see him rejecting of the Cross what he rejected against himself to begin with. Yet if I had a nickel for every time someone like Pastor Philip Ryken insisted that Dr. Stott is not an annihilationist, I would be very rich. He succinctly replaces eternal sin-bearing with a unique exhibition of holy love, which is a moral display of divine love. See how Dr. Stott transmuted "eternal sin-bearing" into "suffer with us" ("misfortune"), as was

---

[34] Dockery, *Holman Bible Handbook* "Moral Display"
[35] WGT Shedd, *The Doctrine of Endless Punishment.*, www.ntslibrary.com, 5
[36] Stott, *The Cross of Christ*, 329-330

prophesied in the second quote. In reply, we already saw the phrase "eternal redemption" in Hebrews 9:12 on page 39. Jesus was required to pay eternally for our sins to ransom them. "... the ransom for a life is costly, no payment is ever enough ..." (Psalms 49:8, NIV). Only sinless eternal sin-bearing could pay for eternal sin. "And if any mischief follow, then thou shalt give life for life" (Exodus 21:23). Therefore, there are scriptures that demand eternal payment for salvation.

I think that Mrs. Eareckson-Tada would be grateful for me defending her belief that Jesus was punished for her eternal sins and healing. But there is no "eternal sin-bearing" or *paralysis-bearing* here. Dr. Stott only cures psychological "restlessness" with "deep comfort".

16. Joni's supposed unique exhibition.

Take Joni Eareckson as an example. ... She has told her story with affecting honesty, including her times of bitterness, anger, rebellion and despair, and how gradually, through the love of her family and friends, she came to trust the sovereignty of God and to build a new life of mouth-painting and public speaking under the signal blessing of God. One night, about three progressive years after her accident, Cindy one of her closest friends, sitting by her bedside, spoke to her of Jesus, saying, "Why, he was paralyzed too." It had not occurred to her before that on the cross Jesus was in similar pain to hers, unable to move, virtually paralyzed. She found this thought deeply comforting.[37]

This narcissistic, moral display of suffering is more requirement than freedom. He has relegated Joni to nothing other than a meaningless poster-child moral-display false Christ.

---

[37] Ibid, 315

E) Physical Atonement. This next quote rejects paralysis-bearing (for example).

> 17. No healing in atonement.
> Sickness may itself be a penalty for sin, but it is not itself a misdemeanor which attracts a penalty. So to speak of Christ "atoning for" our sicknesses is to mix categories; it is not an intelligible notion. [38]

Jesus healed us. "Who his own self bare our sins in his own body on the tree, that we, being dead to sins, should live unto righteousness: by whose stripes ye were healed" (1 Peter 2:24). Healing was in the atonement. "In all their affliction he was afflicted, and the angel of his presence saved them: in his love and in his pity he redeemed them; and he bare them, and carried them all the days of old" (Isaiah 63:9). He bore our grief ("sicknesses"). "Surely he hath borne our griefs, and carried our sorrows: yet we did esteem him stricken, smitten of God, and afflicted" (Isaiah 53:4).

That Christ atoned for spiritual sin and not its physical penalty is unintelligible. Cessationists imply that Jesus became a substitute "spiritual" sinner when they deny substitutional healing. Where is this doctrine that we are not healed now? "There is therefore now no condemnation to them which are in Christ Jesus, who walk not after the flesh, but after the Spirit" (Romans 8:1). Dr. Stott substitutionally voids physical redemption. "And not only they, but ourselves also, which have the firstfruits of the Spirit, even we ourselves groan within ourselves, waiting for the adoption, to wit, the redemption of our body" (Romans 8:23).

F) Substitutionary Eternal Conscious Torment. So that his false father did not physically bare our eternal sin, he twists the Cross into a "satisfaction" of annihilation. Compare

---

[38] Ibid., 245

his direct defense of annihilationism, the first quote, with his argument for it on the Cross, the second quote.

18. Direct annihilationism argument.
The fire itself is termed "eternal" and "unquenchable," but it would be very odd if what is thrown into it proves indestructable. Our expectation would be the opposite: it would be consumed forever, not tormented forever. Hence it is smoke (evidence that the fire has done its work) which "rises for ever and ever" (Revelation 14:11; cf. 19:3).[39]

19. Annihilationism on *The Cross of Christ.*
There is something in God's essential moral being which is "provoked" by evil, and which is "ignited" by it, proceeding to burn until the evil is "consumed" ... Thirdly, there is *the language of satisfaction itself* ... The chief word is *kalah*, which is used particularly by Ezekiel in relation to God's anger ... It occurs in a variety of contexts in the Old Testament, nearly always to indicate the "end" of something, either because it has been destroyed, or because it has finished in some other way. Time, work and life all have an end ...[40]

Notice how he replaced the word "torment" with "consumed" in his direct defense of annihilationism. "And the smoke of their torment ascendeth up for ever and ever: and they have no rest day nor night, who worship the beast and his image, and whosoever receiveth the mark of his name" (Revelation 14:11). He holds Scripture in unrighteousness. "For the wrath of God is revealed from heaven against all ungodliness and

---

[39] Stott, *Evangelical Essentials*, 316
[40] Stott, *The Cross of Christ*, 125-126

unrighteousness of men, who hold the truth in unrighteousness" (Romans 1:18).

Instead of eternal "satisfaction" of moral justice to the Father, he uses the same words – consume and destroy – as in the first quote -- only against his soulless beast-father that "perished." Evangelicals swear by his "masterpiece," *The Cross of Christ*, which teaches annihilation on the Cross. This was not subtitutionary annihilation. "And about the ninth hour Jesus cried with a loud voice, saying, Eli, Eli, lama sabachthani? that is to say, My God, my God, why hast thou forsaken me?" (Matthew 27:46). Since his perceived threat is annihilation, his perceived formulation is annihilation substitution, even though it is an oxymoronic false security.

G) Communion. Christ's true sacrifice was enough to save us by itself. "When Jesus therefore had received the vinegar, he said, It is finished: and he bowed his head, and gave up the ghost" (John 19:30). And faith is our knowledge of the fact that it did save us. "And ye shall know the truth, and the truth shall make you free" (John 8:32). But Dr. Stott himself denies all significance to his other formulations (patripassianism, moral display, and substitutionary annihilation).

> 20. Requires Communion for salvation.
> ... so it was not enough for him to die, but they had to appropriate the benefits of his death personally [through Lord's Supper] ... I used to imagine that because Christ had died, the world had automatically been put right. When someone explained to me that Christ had died for me, I responded rather haughtily "everybody knows that," as if the fact itself or my knowledge of the fact had brought me salvation.[41]

"It was not enough for" Dr. Stott's false father "to die." He came to realize that he was haughty to accept the gospel

---

[41] Ibid., 70-71

message. "… as if the fact itself … had brought me salvation." But communion (additional sacrifice) does not save. "If they shall fall away, to renew them again unto repentance; seeing they crucify to themselves the Son of God afresh, and put him to an open shame" (Hebrews 6:6). Instead, we must remember the finished atonement. "But he that lacketh these things is blind, and cannot see afar off, and hath forgotten that he was purged from his old sins" (2 Peter 1:9).

> ### 21. More work required after the atonement.
> "We are not suggesting that there is nothing left for us to do." [42]

Yet, salvation is by grace alone. "And if by grace, then is it no more of works: otherwise grace is no more grace. But if it be of [finite] works, then is it no more [infinite] grace: otherwise work is no more work" (Romans 11:6). Righteousness is for him that worketh not. "But to him that worketh not, but believeth on him that justifieth the ungodly, his faith is counted for righteousness" (Romans 4:5). We are eternally finished from saving ourselves by the true atonement. "For he that is entered into his rest, he also hath ceased from his own works, as God did from his" (Hebrews 4:10).

---

[42] Stott, *Basic Christianity*, 93

Original Sin	Justification
John 3:6 That which is born of the flesh is flesh;	and that which is born of the Spirit is spirit.
Romans 4:25 … who was delivered up because of our offenses	and was raised again because of our justification (NKJV).
Romans 5:15 But not as the offence, so also is the free gift. For if through the offence of one many be dead,	much more the grace of God, and the gift by grace, which is by one man, Jesus Christ, hath abounded unto many.
Romans 5:16 And not as it was by one that sinned, so is the gift: for the judgment was by one to condemnation,	but the free gift is of many offences unto justification.
Romans 5:17 For if by one man's offence death reigned by one;	much more they which receive abundance of grace and of the gift of righteousness shall reign in life by one, Jesus Christ.
Romans 5:18 Therefore as by the offence of one judgment came upon all men to condemnation;	even so by the righteousness of one the free gift came upon all men unto justification of life.
Romans 5:19 For as by one man's disobedience many were made sinners,	so by the obedience of one shall many be made righteous.

V. ETERNAL SOLA FIDE

A) Pardon from the Cross. It was prophesied long before me that annihilationism's impenitentness disallows pardon because it transmutes sin into a moral process.

> The rejection of the doctrine of Endless Punishment cuts the ground from under the gospel. Salvation supposes a prior damnation. He who denies that he deserves eternal death cannot be saved from it so long as he persists in his denial... the error prevents penitence for sin, and this prevents pardon [acquittal].[43]

22. No pardon from Sacrifice.
Nor, as we have seen, has Christ by his sacrifice prevailed upon God to pardon us.[44]

No, this is not a "new teaching," and I am not a "hyper-Calvinist" nor am I on a hobby horse. I do not hate Dr. Stott nor do I love hell. This quote amounts to Dr. Stott's guaranteed eternal damnation because of his denial of the forgiveness of his sins. And as you can see, Dr. Stott and I are in complete agreement. It is impossible to accuse me of an ad homonym with logic and quotes like these. He insists that he is not delivered from, nor has he escaped from, what he denies. As he rejects heaven and that he was pardoned by the atonement, and as he rejects eternal sin, he is therefore an annihilationist.

B) Have I Swallowed a Camel? Can we confirm that Dr. Stott rejects evangelical pardon? Earlier, Dr. Horton agreed with the above quote by Shedd, that justification (pardon) depends upon a confession of original sin (penitence). Then we saw Dr. Stott limit sin to the self-justifying "infused moral

---

[43] Shedd, *The Doctrine of Endless Punishment.*, 5
[44] Stott, *The Cross of Christ*, 173

process" of "law-breaking" against Adam's original sin. Here is more confirmation that he denies infinite and absolute pardon.

> Jesus said that he who does not believe stands condemned already, just as the one who believes has passed from death unto life. Where is the process that leads to <u>acquittal</u> [pardon]? From the mouth of our Lord and his apostles, the justification is as declarative as the condemnation. If the opposite of justification is judgment – a legal verdict [from heaven], <u>justification cannot be a moral process, but a legal declaration.</u>[45]

> ### 23. No declared righteousness.
> When God <u>justifies sinners, he is not declaring bad people to be good,</u> or saying that they are not sinners after all [...][46]

But pardon is a legal declaration. "And he is entirely fair and just in this present time when he declares sinners to be right in his sight because they believe in Jesus" (Romans 3:26, NLT). We are not reckoned as sinners even as we continue sinning. "Blessed are they whose iniquities are forgiven, and whose sins are covered. Blessed is the man to whom the Lord will not impute sin" (Romans 4:5-8). It is impossible for Dr. Stott to affirm declared righteousness with his impenitent denial of moral justice and original sin. He did not even accept that we are "bad people" who suffer from moral anemia. Dr. Stott is at odds with Dr. Horton, not me. It is not I who has been straining gnats. Dr. Stott and I are in total agreement here.

If I owe infinite dollars (-$∞) and someone else pays zero dollars (+$0) for me, I will not reap infinite credit (+$∞), but I will go to infinite jail (-∞). Likewise, if I reject the infinite riches of Christ, I will also reject the infinite debt. "For ye know the grace of our Lord Jesus Christ, that,

---

[45] Horton, "Justification, Vital Now & Always"
[46] Stott, *The Cross of Christ,* Ibid., 190

though he was rich, yet for your sakes he became poor, that ye through his poverty might be rich" (2 Corinthians 8:9). Annihilationism contradicts saving declared righteousnesss both in truth and in fact.

C) Sola Fide is Essential. Martin Luther taught the deciding doctrine of salvation: "Sola Fide." Justification was salvation. "For therein is the righteousness of God revealed from faith to faith: as it is written, The just shall (eternally) live by faith" (Romans 1:17). Jesus saved us from the wrath to come. "And to wait for his Son from heaven, whom he raised from the dead, even Jesus, which delivered us from the wrath to come" (1 Thessalonians 1:10). Here is Dr. Stott making himself incontrovertibly clear about his rejection of pardon and declared righteousness and justification by faith alone for the third time.

> "Justification by faith alone is the article upon which the church and individual stands or falls." (Luther).

24. Sola Fide rejected.
It would be entirely mistaken to make the equation "salvation equals justification [by faith alone]."[47]

With these last three decisive quotes from Dr. Stott, thus endeth the lesson on the question of his salvation, and he has disannulled it along with sin and the atonement that he may be righteous. "Wilt thou also disannul my judgment? wilt thou condemn me, that thou mayest be righteous?" (Job 40:8). Dr. J.I. Packer's precious Evangelical Annihilationsim and fake friends are fallen from grace. "Christ is become of no effect unto you, whosoever of you are justified by the law; ye are fallen from grace" (Galatians 5:4).

---

[47] Ibid., 188

But again, let him [the sinner] be told, as Scripture teaches, that he was estranged from God by sin, an heir of wrath, exposed to the curse of eternal death, excluded from all hope of salvation, a complete alien from the blessing of God, the slave of Satan, captive under the yoke of sin; in fine, doomed to horrible destruction, and already involved in it; that then Christ interposed, took the punishment upon himself and bore what by the just judgment of God was impending over sinners; with his own blood expiated the sins which rendered them hateful to God, by this expiation satisfied and duly propitiated God the Father, by this intercession appeased his anger, on this basis founded peace between God and men, and by this tie secured the Divine benevolence toward them; will not these considerations move him the more deeply, the more strikingly they represent the greatness of the [eternal] calamity from which he was delivered?[48]

But even if we or an angel from heaven should preach a Gospel other than the one we preached to you, let him be eternally condemned! As we have already said, so now I say again: If anybody is preaching to you a Gospel other than what you accepted, let him be eternally condemned! (Galatians 1:8-9, NIV).

---

[48] Calvin, *Institutes*, II.16.2

Adam incurred an infinite debt (Job 22:5).	Would there not, then, be a serious disproportion between sins consciously committed in time and torment consciously experienced throughout eternity?[49]
Sin is eternally punished (2 Thessalonians 1:9).	For [negative] example, " ... if you put your hand in the fire it will be burnt, and if you break the Ten Commandments you will [not] be punished"[50]
Eternal sin-bearing (Hebrews 9:12)	Christ bore our sins and died our death because of his love and justice, we must not think of it as expressing eternal sin-bearing in the heart of God.[51]
Jesus was punished for our sins (1 Peter 3:18).	Crude interpretations of the cross still emerge in some of our evangelical illustrations. ... when we portray him as the whipping-boy who is punished instead of the real culprit.[52]
Jesus pardons (Micah 7:18).	Nor, as we have seen, has Christ by his sacrifice prevailed upon God to pardon us.[53]
God declares sinners right (Romans 3:26).	When God justifies sinners, he is not declaring bad people to be good, or saying that they are not sinners after all ... [54]
Justification is salvation (Galatians 3:11).	It would be entirely mistaken to make the equation "salvation equals justification [by faith alone]."[55]

[49] Stott, *Evangelical Essentials*, 318.
[50] Stott, *The Cross of Christ*, 116
[51] Ibid., 329-330.
[52] Ibid., 150.
[53] Ibid., 173.
[54] Ibid., 190
[55] Ibid., 188.

E) Justification and Inspiration and Inerrancy.
Remember how I showed at the beginning that all Scripture is
eternal? Dr. Stott also denies the eternal inspiration and
inerrancy of Scripture, which further denies faith alone. In this
next quote, he is saying that Paul was finitely humanly authoring
scripture.

> 24. Uninspired and errant gospel.
> [We] have sometimes been incautious in our
> phraseology [of liberty], and have given the
> impression that good works are of no
> importance. But then the apostle Paul could
> evidently be incautious too, since his critics [like
> the Roman Catholics] flung exactly the same
> charge against him, which led him to cry: "What
> shall we say, then? Shall we go on sinning, so that
> grace may increase?" (Romans 6:1). ... [56]

The Judaizers, his critics, like the Roman Catholics often
criticize the Protestants, rebuked him to repent of his faith alone
and liberty, which were supposedly "incautious," by inserting
Romans 6:1 for "important" good works in addition to liberty.
But he does not understand that would make the gospel both
uninspired and errant.

> "Knowing this first, that no prophecy of the
> scripture is of any private interpretation. For the
> prophecy came not in old time by the will of
> man: but holy men of God spake as they were
> moved by the Holy Ghost. But there were false
> prophets also among the people, even as there
> shall be false teachers among you, who privily
> shall bring in damnable heresies, even denying
> the Lord that bought them, and bring upon
> themselves swift destruction. And many shall
> follow their pernicious ways; by reason of whom

[56] Ibid., 187-188

the way of truth shall be evil spoken of. And through covetousness shall they with feigned words make merchandise of you: whose judgment now of a long time lingereth not, and their damnation slumbereth not" (2 Peter 1:20-21; 2:1-3).

Both Dr. Stott and his errant, uninspired, human heretical authors of Holy Writ reject Sola Fide. But the Word of God and Sola Fide within it are both inspired and eternal. The feigned words of existentialism explain why the modern Reformation follows the pernicious ways of evangelical annihilationists, and their damnation slumbereth not.

F) Nietzsche accepted Scripture. Unlike Dr. Stott, the infamous atheist Fredrick Nietzsche was convinced that justification by faith alone was Paul's true message in scripture itself. (He did not conclude that Romans 6:1 negated it). But then he argued that all Scripture was delusional and weak. He mocks Paul's struggle with his conscience about the eternal Law.

And ... moments came when he said to himself: "It is all in vain; the torture of the unfulfilled law cannot be overcome" ... The law was the cross to which he felt himself nailed: how he hated it! How he searched for some means to annihilate it – not to fulfill it any more himself! And finally the saving thought struck him, "It is unreasonable to persecute this Jesus! Here after all is the way out; here is the perfect revenge; here and nowhere else I have and hold the annihilator of the law! Until then the ignominious death had seemed to him the chief argument against the Messianic claim of which the new doctrine spoke: but what if it were necessary to get rid of the law[57]

He said that Paul's Jesus was a rebellious false messiah and that His death was the end of His zeal against the Pharisees. Nietzsche's false Paul then spurred on the rebellion after Jesus suffered capital punishment by selling his converts on a false resurrection and lawlessness. But above, unlike Nietzsche, we saw how Dr. Stott simply perniciously wrote Romans 6:1 into Scripture for good deeds, against faith alone, by the Judaizers.

G) Three Examples of Legalism. Firstly, the Law is not sociological. "Jesus said unto him, Thou shalt love the Lord thy God with all thy heart, and with all thy soul, and with all thy mind" (Matthew 22:37). We have sinned against God and not only man. "For all have sinned, and come short of the glory of God" (Romans 3:23). What exactly are Dr. Stott's self-justifying moral processes? They are revamped law-breaking. Even if they make sense to the human mind, these next three finite alternative "processes do not lead to acquittal" from eternal condemnation. These are his human alternatives to faith:

26. & 27. & 28. Legalistic moral processes.

It is easy to write this condemnation of social relationships today. ... If only the spirit of self-assertion could be replaced by the spirit of self-sacrifice, our conflicts would cease. ...[58]
Forgiveness signals an approach to wrong in terms, not of peace at any price, nor of a destructive intention to destroy the wrongdoer, but of a willingness to seek to reshape the future in the light of the wrong, in the most creative way possible. [59]

---

[57] Fredrick Nietzsche, R.J. Hollingdale transl, *Daybreak*. (Cambridge University Press Cambridge, 1987) Page 68

[58] Stott, *The Cross of Christ*, 79-80

[59] Ibid, 310

> They had learnt that the servant was not greater
> than the master [sic], and that for them as for
> him suffering was the means to glory. More
> than that, suffering *was* [his italics] glory ...[60]

These three philosophies do not pay for the infinite debt
like true, infinite, declared righteousness. "Self-assertion" is
another example of "law-breaking." And "self-sacrifice" would
replace Jesus Christ's self-sacrifice on our behalf. Dr.
Stott might be solving earthly problems like depression, but not the eternal
great gulf. Lot's wife self-sacrificed for homosexuals. "But his
wife looked back from behind him, and she became a pillar of
salt" (Genesis 19:26).

Finite "creativity" would be easy but for our moral
anemia. "Lo, this only have I found, that God hath made man
upright; but they have sought out many inventions" (Ecclesiastes
7:29). Our "creativity" must be eternal to accomplish eternal
"forgiveness." And I don't see much hope here for Joni if
"suffering is glory" instead of healing and redemption. Jesus did
not believe that suffering itself was glorious even though He
died for the Church. "Let nothing be done through strife or
vainglory; but in lowliness of mind let each esteem others better
than themselves" (Philippians 2:3).

Annihilationists turn salvation itself into eternal
conscious suffering through works-righteousness. And eternal
life does not come from good deeds. "Not of works, lest any
man should boast" (Ephesians 2:9). Our suffering and striving
will not profit us. "I will declare thy righteousness, and thy
works; for they shall not profit thee" (Isaiah 57:12). Good deeds
are filthy rags. "But we are all as an unclean thing, and all our
righteousnesses are as filthy rags; and we all do fade as a leaf; and
our iniquities, like the wind, have taken us away" (Isaiah 64:6).

H) Intro to the Will to Power. Nietzsche, who we saw
denied faith alone, waged a similar legalistic moral process war

---

[60] Ibid, 40

against Christianity. Like Freud's "libido," the "will-to-power" was Nietzsche's psychiatric solution to Paul's pricked conscience over the infinite debt.

> Suppose, finally, we succeeded in explaining our entire instinctive life as the development and ramification of one basic form of the will -- namely, of the will-to-power, as my proposition has it ... then one would have gained the right to determine all efficient force univocally as will-to-power. The world viewed from inside ... it would be "will-to-power" and nothing else.[61]

Compare this language to the above three Stott moral processes. It is another, fourth, finite, moral process, legalistic philosophy. Supposedly, all Paul and we need to do is remember our internal willpower to achieve immortality. Grace is not human will-to-power. "For by grace are ye saved through faith; and that not of yourselves: it is the gift of God: Not of works, lest any man should boast" (Ephesians 2:8-9). Eternal salvation is not by will. "So then it is not of him that willeth, nor of him that runneth, but of God that sheweth mercy" (Romans 9:16). It is not by power. "Then he answered and spake unto me, saying, This is the word of the LORD unto Zerubbabel, saying, Not by might, nor by power, but by my spirit, saith the LORD of hosts" (Zechariah 4:6). Neither Stott nor Nietzsche knows that they have sinned against eternal life and are, therefore, under an eternal curse. We will see how Dr. Stott also endorses Nietzsche's moral process.

G) Eternal Salvation. The conclusion is that annihilationists do not accept eternal sinlessness. "Come now, and let us reason together, saith the LORD: though your sins be as scarlet, they shall be as white as snow; though they be red like crimson, they shall be as wool" (Isaiah 1:18). They do not

---

[61] Nietzsche, Walter Kaufmann transl, *Beyond Good and Evil*, (Vintage, 1989), 36

believe in eternal forgiveness. "As far as the east is from the west, so far hath he removed our transgressions from us" (Psalms 103:12). They attack eternal righteousness. "Seventy weeks are determined upon thy people and upon thy holy city, to finish the transgression, and to make an end of sins, and to make reconciliation for iniquity, and to bring in everlasting righteousness, and to seal up the vision and prophecy, and to anoint the most Holy" (Daniel 9:24). Annihilationists deny God's eternal mercy.

> "O give thanks unto the LORD; for he is good: because his mercy endureth for ever. Let Israel now say, that his mercy endureth for ever. Let the house of Aaron now say, that his mercy endureth for ever. Let them now that fear the LORD say, that his mercy endureth for ever" (Psalms 118:1-4).

But mercy that endures forever is the everlasting covenant. "Nevertheless I will remember my covenant with thee in the days of thy youth, and I will establish unto thee an everlasting covenant" (Ezekiel 16:60). It is the everlasting gospel. "And I saw another angel fly in the midst of heaven, having the everlasting gospel to preach unto them that dwell on the earth, and to every nation, and kindred, and tongue, and people" (Revelation 14:6). It is everlasting salvation. "But Israel shall be saved in the LORD with an everlasting salvation: ye shall not be ashamed nor confounded world without end" (Isaiah 45:17). It is everlasting joy. "And the ransomed of the LORD shall return, and come to Zion with songs and everlasting joy upon their heads: they shall obtain joy and gladness, and sorrow and sighing shall flee away" (Isaiah 35:10). It is the everlasting kingdom. "For so an entrance shall be ministered unto you abundantly into the everlasting kingdom of our Lord and Saviour Jesus Christ" (2 Peter 1:11). It is everlasting life. "Verily, verily, I say unto you, He that believeth on me hath everlasting life" (John 6:47). But as we have seen, Dr. Stott rejects eternal life and

justification.   Will   he   now   affirm   a   reasonable   model   of
sanctification?

VI. THE RESURRECTION AND PROMISES

A) Raised because of Our Justification. Christ
humbly submitted to our instant eternal torment. "He was
oppressed, and he was afflicted, yet he opened not his mouth: he
is brought as a lamb to the slaughter, and as a sheep before her
shearers is dumb, so he openeth not his mouth" (Isaiah 53:7).
But instead of Dr. Stott's beast-father submissively paying for
our eternal sins to God, it literally "masters" (defeats) a human
cross. His false cross was only the wrath of man.

> 29. The father- beast rejects atonement for sin.
> As he was suspended there, bound hand and foot
> to the wood in apparent weakness, they imagined
> they had him at their mercy, and flung
> themselves upon him with hostile intent ...
> [Stott's ellipses] But he grappled with them and
> mastered them. [62]

> 30. Impromptu antichrist resuscitation.
> Indeed, the reason for emphasizing the
> resurrection may be rather to emphasize
> something about the death which it cancels and
> conquers ... In other words, the resurrection was
> the divine reversal of the human verdict. [63]

Then, he deceptively switches the focus from mastering
human wrath onto a non sequitur existential beast's
resuscitation. "And deceiveth them that dwell on the earth by
the means of those miracles which he had power to do in the
sight of the beast; saying to them that dwell on the earth, that
they should make an image to the beast, which had the wound

---

[62] Ibid, 235
[63] Ibid, 35

[death] by a sword, and did live [resuscitates]" (Revelation 13:14). His antichrist beast "cancels," "conquers" and "reverses" the wrath of man by magically resuscitating, instead of paying for sins. The world only thinks in terms of power and war, not forgiveness from God. It is deceived by this antichrist, death-defying, naturalistic, willpower resuscitation. "And they worshipped the dragon, because he gave his authority unto the beast; and they worshipped the beast, saying, Who is like unto the beast? And who is able to war with him?" (Revelation 13:4).

But for believers, the true Jesus Christ was raised from the dead because He submitted to sinless eternal substitution. "Who was delivered up because of our offenses, and was raised because of our justification" (Romans 4:25, NKJV). His true eternal resurrection revolved around the atonement. "For if, when we were enemies, we were reconciled to God by the death of his Son, much more, being reconciled, we shall be saved by his life. And not only so, but we also joy in God through our Lord Jesus Christ, by whom we have now received the atonement" (Romans 5:10-11). The resurrection was only a "moral display" of His prior sinless submission to death. "Jesus saith unto him, Thomas, because thou hast seen me, thou hast believed: blessed are they that have not seen, and yet have believed" (John 20:29). And so Dr. Stott does not understand or believe in the eternal resurrection.

B) Regeneration and Pardon. But true born-again power is God's pardon. "For the preaching of the cross is to them that perish foolishness; but unto us which are saved it is the power of God" (1 Corinthians 1:18). It is not by good works, but by the Spirit. "Not by works of righteousness which we have done, but according to his mercy he saved us, by the washing of regeneration, and renewing of the Holy Ghost" (Titus 3:5). Instead of new birth, Dr. Stott's imaginative salvation is being psychoanalytically united to his resuscitated beast. His context for this false, carnal, "inward" vigor is to *deny* God's miraculous healing. Calvin said earlier, in his defence of immortality and conversion, that the mere knowledge of God sufficiently proves that souls that rise higher than the world must be immortal, it being impossible that any [finite] evanescent vigour could reach the very fountain of life.

31. No inward spiritual regeneration.

Even when we are feeling tired, sick and battered, we experience a [evanescent] vigor and vitality which are the life of the risen [resuscitated] Jesus within us. Paul expresses the same thought in verse [2 Corinthians 4:16]: "Though outwardly we are wasting away, yet inwardly we are being renewed day by day." ... The life of Jesus ... [is] the human body['s] marvelous therapeutic processes which fight disease and restore health ...[64]

But *The People's New Testament Commentary* by B.W. Johnson says about 2 Corinthians 4:16 that "His spiritual strength is constantly renewed by Christ. The 'inward man' is the immaterial nature in contrast with the material body." All spirituality is eternal. But Dr. Stott's secret, "inward" heart before Jesus is filled with the human body's marvelous, materialistic, therapeutic resuscitation, moral processes for fighting disease and restoring health. The human body's therapeutic processes are how he defines all healing miracles. It is his psychiatric second wind from a false "risen Jesus." Dr. Stott's evanescent hope is as if Lazarus resuscitated, after being four days dead, by his marvelous human body's therapeutic processes, like the movie "Dawn of the Dead."

True regenerate spirituality is not vigor and vitality. "For they that are such serve not our Lord Jesus Christ, but their own belly; and by good words and fair speeches deceive the hearts of the simple" (Romans 16:18). Dr. Stott is not a new spiritual creature. "For in Christ Jesus neither circumcision availeth any thing, nor uncircumcision, but a new creature" (Galatians 6:15).

---

[64] Ibid, 245-246

He denied his secret, inward soul, or God-shaped hole, before Jesus through evolution. Nor did his Jesus-beast have a secret, inward soul for the purposes of its annihilation, to which we were subjected to in detail. And, earlier, Dr. Stott said that Paul's critics authored Romans 6:1 against faith and the Holy Spirit. He does not possess the Holy Spirit. Yet, Dr. Stott is a "master of Israel" for all his new-found inward fleshly vigor.

> "That which is born of the flesh is flesh; and that which is born of the Spirit is spirit. Marvel not that I said unto thee, Ye must be born again. The wind bloweth where it listeth, and thou hearest the sound thereof, but canst not tell whence it cometh, and whither it goeth: so is every one that is born of the Spirit. Nicodemus answered and said unto him, How can these things be? Jesus answered and said unto him, Art thou a master of Israel, and knowest not these things?" (John 3:6-10).

C) Dr. Stott's Warfare. What is the effect of a fleshly regeneration over the leading of the Holy Spirit? In the next quote, Dr. Stott adopts the "will-to-power," carnal moral process into his salvation. Even though he believes in a resurrection, and Nietzsche rejects it, it is a moot point because it is all imaginary anyway. These next prophets of peace are inwardly ravening wolves. "Beware of false prophets, which come to you in sheep's clothing, but inwardly they are ravening wolves" (Matthew 7:15).

32. Will-to-power.
From the life-stories of history's most influential politicians he had made the astonishing discovery that nearly 300 of them were orphans, from Alexander the Great and Julius Caesar through Charles V and Louis XIV to George

Washington, Napoleon and (less happily) Lenin, Hitler, Stalin and Castro. This naturally struck Dr. Touriner, since he had long lectured on the importance for the child's development of a mother and father performing their roles harmoniously -- which is exactly what the most influential politicians never had! Dr. Rentchnik developed a theory that "the insecurity consequent upon emotional depravation must have aroused in these children an exceptional will-to-power." The same was evidently true of religious leaders, since for example, Moses, the Buddha, Confucious, and Mohammed were also all orphans. Professor Andre Haynal, a psychoanalyst, has worked further on the theory, and suggests that "depravation" of any kind (not just being orphaned) lie behind creativity (which he prefers to "will-to-power").[65]

This quote is devoid of all mention of God or Scripture or famous Christian leaders. Instead, it is a list of the most infamous, antichrist, "influential politicians" and "religious leaders" of all time. "For there are certain men crept in unawares, who were before of old ordained to this condemnation, ungodly men, turning the grace of our God into lasciviousness, and denying the only Lord God, and our Lord Jesus Christ" (Jude 4). Compare the "suffering *was* glory" with "when we are feeling tired, sick and battered, we experience a vigor and vitality" and "emotional depravation must have aroused in these children an exceptional will-to-power." Contrast this self-justifying moral processes with "And not only so, but we glory in tribulations also: knowing that tribulation worketh patience; And patience, experience; and experience, hope" (Romans 5:3-4).

In other words, it seems to be disgruntlement. He teaches on the "insecurities" instead of peace and assurance.

---

[65] Stott, *The Cross of Christ* , 319

"And the work of [declared] righteousness shall be peace; and the effect of righteousness quietness and assurance for ever" (Isaiah 32:17). Here are his insecurities. "But a certain fearful looking for of judgment and fiery indignation, which shall devour the adversaries" (Hebrews 10:27). Apparently, being raised by parents indicates that you aren't saved? "Backbiters, haters of God, despiteful, proud, boasters, inventors of evil things, disobedient to parents" (Romans 1:30). Criminal, soulless psychiatry has produced orphans from hell. "Woe unto you, scribes and Pharisees, hypocrites! for ye compass sea and land to make one proselyte, and when he is made, ye make him twofold more the child of hell than yourselves" (Matthew 23:15).

Charles V launched the Counter Reformation. Why is George Washington on this list? I hope that Joni's insecurities don't arouse in her a "new life of mouth painting" and genocide. Will you now follow Stalin, Hitler and Castro (who were all obsessed with Nietzsche) into hell? "The fool hath said in his heart, There is no God. They are corrupt, they have done abominable works, there is none that doeth good" (Psalms 14:1). While Dr. Stott felt "less happy" to include the Communists, he is not "less happy" to include the false religions. How about following Buddha and Mohammed all the way into your everlasting burnings? "And God spake all these words, saying, I am the LORD thy God, which have brought thee out of the land of Egypt, out of the house of bondage. Thou shalt have no other gods before me" (Exodus 20:2-3).

They are all tyrants. "Yea also, because he transgresseth by wine, he is a proud man, neither keepeth at home, who enlargeth his desire as hell, and is as death, and cannot be satisfied, but gathereth unto him all nations, and heapeth unto him all people" (Habakkuk 2:5). Being born sinners results in heathen warfare against man and God; following after his resuscitated Beast.

> "Why do the heathen rage, and the people imagine a vain thing? The kings of the earth set themselves, and the rulers take counsel together,

against the LORD, and against his anointed, saying, Let us break their bands asunder, and cast away their cords from us. He that sitteth in the heavens shall laugh: the Lord shall have them in derision. Then shall he speak unto them in his wrath, and vex them in his sore displeasure" (Psalms 2:1-5).

D) Moses and the Promises of the Cross. But thank God that Moses defeated the Pharaoh, who fits in better with Hitler and Stalin, by standing on the infinite God's revelation. "That ye be not slothful, but followers of them who through faith and patience inherit the promises" (Hebrews 6:12). By invisible faith in the atonement, not to emphasize the resurrection, as evidenced by the keeping of the Passover, Moses moved in the opposite direction of the 300 orphans, unto suffering at their reproach and received eternal riches of Christ. As for Moses' parents, they supported him.

"By faith Moses, when he was born, was hid three months of his parents, because they saw he was a proper child; and they were not afraid of the king's commandment. By faith Moses, when he was come to years, refused to be called the son of Pharaoh's daughter; Choosing rather to suffer affliction with the people of God, than to enjoy the pleasures of sin for a season; Esteeming the reproach of Christ greater riches than the treasures in Egypt: for he had respect unto the recompence of the reward. By faith he forsook Egypt, not fearing the wrath of the king: for he endured, as seeing him who is invisible. Through faith he kept the passover, and the sprinkling of blood, lest he that destroyed the firstborn should touch them. By faith they passed through the Red sea as by dry land: which the Egyptians assaying to do were drowned" (Hebrews 11:23-29).

But focusing on the resurrection instead of the Cross implies that you prefer willpower over pardon by the blood of Christ, and willpower does not save.

E) False Assurance. Justin Martyr (who is in the next quote) was the first person in recorded Church History to deny the immortality of the soul. He fits in with the 300 orphans because he wore a goofy "philosophers robe" everywhere. "For God hath not given us the spirit of fear; but of power, and of love, and of a sound mind" (2 Timothy 1:7).

33. & 34. False signs of assurance.

> Justin Martyr, the second-century Christian apologist, confessed that wherever he looked, he saw the cross. Neither the sea is crossed nor the earth is ploughed without it, he writes, referring to a ship's mast and yard, and to a plough's blade and yoke. Diggers and mechanics do not work without cross-shaped tools, alluding presumably to a spade and its handle. Moreover, "the human form differs from that of the irrational animals in nothing else than its being erect and having the arms extended." And if the torso and arms of the human form proclaim the cross, so do the nose and eyebrows of the human face. Fanciful? Yes, entirely, yet I find myself willing to forgive any such fancies which glorify the cross ... It was, I know, an obsessive interest. ...[66]

> ... what Thomas said of Christ, the world is saying about the church. And the world is also saying to every preacher: Unless I see in your hands the print of the nails, I will not believe[...][67]

---

[66] Ibid, 45-46
[67] Ibid, 351

Most Christians don't even wear crosses around their necks or have them in their sanctuaries. This is not what it means to be crucified unto the world. "But God forbid that I should glory, save in the cross of our Lord Jesus Christ, by whom the world is crucified unto me, and I unto the world" (Galatians 6:14). These are not images of assurance, but only "emotional deprivation" from self-justification. "They that make a graven image are all of them vanity; and their delectable things shall not profit; and they are their own witnesses; they see not, nor know; that they may be ashamed" (Isaiah 44:9).

VII. THE ETERNAL PERSON AND DEITY OF CHRIST

A) Atonement and Deity. St. Anselm demonstrated that eternal conscious torment is true because Jesus was infinite on the Cross. Here is a modern author rephrasing his *Why God Became Man* in terms of eternal conscious torment.

> If Christ was simply a human, albeit the perfect person ... [He would have only suffered] a finite penalty, such as annihilation, is consistent with that scenario. But Christ was not simply a human ... God himself [besides simply being a perfect human] was present at the cross. For Jesus' cry, "My God, My God, why have you forsaken me?" (Matthew 27:46), is that of the "Lord of glory" (1 Corinthians 2:8) himself, accepting the punishment due us. Jesus' priestly work therefore establishes that the penalty for sin against the infinite must be infinite. Similarly, God's punishment of the damned will be infinite, of everlasting duration. [68]

---

[68] Timothy Phillips, edited by William Crocket and James Sigountos, "Hell: A Christological Reflection," *Through No Fault of Their Own?*, (Baker Publishing Group, 1991) 53

Dr. Phillips also intends that this infinity is a QUANTITATIVE "DURATION" when he distinguishes it from mere qualitative perfection. There is a distinction between a perfect heaven and an infinite heaven. He went on: "Only the [infinite] God-man could establish this reconciliation... It is no accident that, historically, annihilationism has gone hand in hand with the denial of Jesus' [infinite] deity."[69]

Dr. Stott knows that deity implies infinity. And he rejected pardon and reconciliation, because it implies the infinite debt. Hence, it is no accident that, along with reconciliation, Dr. Stott must also deny the *infinite* deity of Christ.

35. Denial of Deity of Christ.

It would be wiser instead to say what the New Testament authors said, faithfully echoed by the Apostles' Creed, namely that he who "was conceived by the Holy Spirit, born of the Virgin Mary, suffered under Pontius Pilate, was crucified, died and buried" was not "God."[70]

Did the "New Testament authors" really deny the deity of Christ? Jesus is the true God. "And we know that the Son of God is come, and hath given us an understanding, that we may know him that is true, and we are in him that is true, even in his Son Jesus Christ. This is the true God, and eternal life" (1 John 5:20). Jesus is God forever and ever. "But unto the Son he saith, Thy throne, O God, is for ever and ever: a sceptre of righteousness is the sceptre of thy kingdom" (Hebrews 1:8).

"The Apostles Creed" did not deny the deity of Christ.

I believe in God, the Father Almighty, the Creator of heaven and earth, and in Jesus Christ, His only Son, our Lord: Who was conceived of the Holy Spirit, born of the Virgin Mary, suffered

---

[69] Ibid, 53
[70] Stott, *The Cross of Christ*, 156

under Pontius Pilate, was crucified, died, and was
buried. He descended into hell. The third day He
arose again from the dead. He ascended into
heaven and sits at the right hand of God the
Father Almighty, whence He shall come to judge
the living and the dead. I believe in the Holy
Spirit, the holy catholic church, the communion
of saints, the forgiveness of sins, the resurrection
of the body, and life everlasting. Amen. [71]

Compare the true "Who was conceived" with his
cropped "he who 'was conceived ...'" He systematically
annihilates the infinite God of infinite heaven so there can be no
a priori infinite moral justice nor any infinite reconciliation.

B) Atonement and Christology. What is the "context"
for "he who 'was conceived by the Holy Spirit' ... was not
God"? I already showed you three quotes of him replacing the
Son with the Father so that there was no punishment on the
Cross. Here "it seems permissible" to him that the Person of
Jesus was a downward morph, or the "modalism" of Oneness
Pentecostalism, of a descended false father into the Virgin.

<u>36. & 37. & 38. Patripassianism/modalism.</u>

> ... the critics of Praxeas' followers to give them
> the nickname "Patripassians" ... [but] since
> Jesus was both God [of Patripassianism] and
> man, the Council of Ephesus (AD 431)
> declared it correct to refer to the Virgin Mary as
> theotokos ("mother of God [the father])-",
> literally "God-bearer"). Similarly, and for the
> same reason, it seems permissible to refer to
> God [the father] suffering on the cross. For

[71] *Apostles' Creed*
[72] Stott, *The Cross of Christ*, 155-156

> God could be born, why could he not die?[72]
>
> [Jesus is] ... Not God as he is in himself (the Father) [his parenthesis], but God nevertheless, God-made-man-in-Christ (the Son).[73]
>
> God himself, the Father, was on the cross [only named] of Jesus.[74]
>
> [a reprint] There is no question now of the Father inflicting punishment on the Son or of the Son intervening on our behalf with the Father, for it is the Father himself who takes the initiative in his love, bears the penalty of sin himself, and so dies.[75]

It seems that when he sees John 3:16, he thinks that "God" is NOT the common divinity for the separate Person of God the Father and God the Son and God the Holy Ghost. Throughout his illustrious career, even as one of the editors of *Christianity Today,* he still thinks today that "God" can only be the PERSON of the Father for all of Scripture. He believes that the Father existentially *"substituted himself"*[76] down in the flesh renamed the Son, instead of sending the true Son in the flesh. "And every spirit that confesseth not that Jesus Christ is come in the flesh is not of God: and this is that spirit of antichrist, whereof ye have heard that it should come; and even now already is it in the world" (1 John 4:3). He does not conceive of the Son being a separate eternally-existing person from the Father and possessing the same DEITY. This is his existential definition of "substitution" down from heaven not up to the true Father in heaven. The reason why his false Jesus "was not God" nor "the Father" is because his Jesus was only the soulless beast that his false virgin contributed to his finite false father.

---

[73] Ibid, 158
[74] Ibid, 334
[75] Ibid., 152
[76] Ibid, 160

Therefore, we have learned that the Trinity depends upon penal substitution, and that depends upon eternal conscious torment.

He has not come to the true saving Father without Christ. "Jesus saith unto him, I am the way, the truth, and the life: no man cometh unto the Father, but by me" (John 14:6). He has even annihilated the Father. He transgresses against both the Father and Son. "Whosoever transgresseth, and abideth not in the doctrine of Christ, hath not [rejects] God. He that abideth in the doctrine of Christ, he hath both the Father and the Son. If there come any unto you, and bring not this doctrine, receive him not into your house, neither bid him God speed" (2 John 1:9-10). His god has no soul, and he does not exist, which is displeasing (Hebrews 11:6). He has uttered Christ's name in vain, and it is a name without a reality. Dr. Stott has annihilated every aspect of salvation and the gospel including the person, deity and work of Christ. He has systematically annihilated everything and everyone but Hitler, Stalin, Nietzsche, Buddha and Mohammed.

> His Word surely abides forever and, if it does, sinners abide in hell forever. If they are ever annihilated, He and His word are annihilated with them. This is the reason why I wrote this book. Not because I love hell and hate annihilation, but because I hate attempts to annihilate God and His Son, Jesus Christ.[77]

---

[77] John Gerstner, *Repent or Perish*, (Orlando: Soli Deo Gloria/Ligonier Ministries, 1996), 185

Uninspired and errant Scripture	But then the apostle Paul could evidently be incautious too, since his critics like the Roman Catholics] flung exactly the same charge against him, which led him to cry: "What shall we say, then? Shall we go on sinning, so that grace may increase?" (Romans 6:1). ... [78]
Carnal new birth	"Though outwardly we are wasting away, yet inwardly we are being renewed day by day." ... The life of Jesus ... [is] the human body['s] marvelous therapeutic processes which fight disease and restore health ...[79]
Hitler, Stalin, Nietzsche, Buddha, Mohammed endorsed	nearly 300 of them were orphans, from Alexander the Great and Julius Caesar through Charles V and Louis XIV to George Washington, Napoleon and (less happily) Lenin, Hitler, Stalin and Castro. This naturally struck Dr. Touriner, since he had long lectured on the importance for the child's development of a mother and father performing their roles harmoniously -- which is exactly what the most influential politicians never had! Dr. Rentchnik developed a theory that "the insecurity consequent upon emotional depravation must have aroused in these children an exceptional will-to-power." The same was evidently true of religious leaders, since for example, Moses, the Buddha, Confucious, and Mohammed. [80]
Jesus was not God	he who "was conceived by the Holy Spirit, born of the Virgin Mary, suffered under Pontius Pilate, was crucified, died and buried" was not "God."[81]
Jesus was not Person	[Jesus is] ... Not God as he is in himself (the Father) [his parenthesis], but God nevertheless, God-made-man-in-Christ (the Son).[82]

---

[78] Stott, *The Cross*, 187-188

[79] Ibid, 245-246

[80] Ibid , 319

[81] Ibid, 156

[82] Ibid, 158

VIII. Conclusion: Eternal Conscious Torment Is Essential For Eternal Life; "In Essentials Unity ... In All Things Charity"

Top Ten Historical And Systematic Excuses For Propagating Dr. Stott's Worldwide Eternal Perdition

10. It's poor word choice.
9. Dr. Stott is refuting heresies beyond your ignorant comprehension.
8. Dr. Stott is not an annihilationist.
7. You are arrogant. (C.J. Mahaney)
6. Dr. Stott is a statesman.
5. The Cross isn't about hell/Faith is not logical, and that is why annihilationists can be saved. (Pastor Chris Coury)
4. I've read plenty of Stott books! (Senior Pastor Chas. W. Lyons)
3. Tell your pastor you have to work on an attitude problem.
2. This is a very poorly written book.
1. You have devoted your life to disproving annihilationism. (Pastor John Thompson)

"HERE I STAND" (LUTHER) DR. STOTT ARGUES AGAINST HIS OWN "ETERNAL SIN," CHRIST'S "ETERNAL SIN-BEARING," AND THAT HE WAS, THEREBY, "PARDONED" AND "DECLARED RIGHTEOUS" IN THE CROSS OF CHRIST! WHO DO THESE DETRACTORS OF MINE AGREE WITH? ARE THEY ALSO FALLEN FROM GRACE? Have I overreacted?

The only thing that matters is winning the "argument" in God's eyes. "For there must be also heresies among you, that they which are approved may be made manifest among you" (1 Corinthians 11:19). I am unashamed. "Study to shew thyself approved unto God, a workman that needeth not to be ashamed, rightly dividing the word of truth" (2 Timothy 2:15).

Historical Orthodoxy is ashamed. "Hear the word of the LORD, ye that tremble at his word; Your brethren that hated you, that cast you out for my name's sake, said, Let the LORD be glorified: but he shall appear to your joy, and they shall be ashamed" (Isaiah 66:5). I will not fellowship with his supporters. "I have hated the congregation of evil doers; and will not sit with the wicked" (Psalms 26:5). But now I have no pastors, teachers or friends left. "And he said, I have been very jealous for the LORD God of hosts: for the children of Israel have forsaken thy covenant, thrown down thine altars, and slain thy prophets with the sword; and I, even I only, am left; and they seek my life, to take it away" (1 Kings 19:10).

This is not a book about hell. This is about the Law-Gospel distinction. And it is not the Gospel-Law distinction. You cannot skip over the full despair and "profess Christ" and then "formulate" eternal conscious torment and the Law and sin. In that case, you are formulating backwards from salvation into hell. Christianity is not about giving your heart to Christ or following Him. It is about the fear of God — with a glorious escape to the Cross, where there is no more formulating hell. "There is no fear in love; but perfect love casteth out fear: because fear hath torment. He that feareth is not made perfect in love" (1 John 4:18). But the Law must precede the Cross for conversion to this love.

And we must do more than "profess Christ" but confess that "Jesus is Lord" over death and hell. The fear of God is the beginning of conversion, not the effect. "The fear of the LORD is the beginning of wisdom: and the knowledge of the holy is understanding" (Proverbs 9:10). There are many leading false formulators of eternal conscious torment within the Church today that never completely "formulate" eternal conscious torment unto conversion. "Ever learning, and never able to come to the knowledge of the truth" (2 Timothy 3:7). Neither Christ nor hell are ideas or concepts. "And the peace of God, which passeth all understanding, shall keep your hearts and minds through Christ Jesus" (Philippians 4:7). Salvation was not a free lunch with hell as an option to think about.

We must separate ourselves from evangelical annihilationsts. "And the seed of Israel separated themselves from all strangers, and stood and confessed their sins, and the iniquities of their fathers" (Nehemiah 9:2). Church history must annihilate legalism. "And the king commanded Hilkiah the high priest, and the priests of the second order, and the keepers of the door, to bring forth out of the temple of the LORD all the vessels that were made for Baal, and for the grove, and for all the host of heaven: and he burned them without Jerusalem in the fields of Kidron, and carried the ashes of them unto Bethel" (2 Kings 23:4).

I am a true and unique friend of Dr. John Stott's, and I love him. If he is humble, I think he will even admit that I served him. I have blown the trumpet and his blood is not at my hands. This has hardly been gossip. Logic and proof do not make for an ad homonym. We will see the same logic without reference to Dr. Stott in C.H. Spurgeon and John Calvin in the articles following. Purgatory and Nirvana fall under this same condemnation of original sin. I have not compared myself to him. This is all theology and no politics or gainsay. Maybe if we pray, he will repent. "Beareth all things, believeth all things, hopeth all things, endureth all things" (1 Corinthians 13:7). I wrote this book for one Linda Piepenbrink. "Wherefore David arose and went, he and his men, and slew of the Philistines two hundred men; and David brought their foreskins, and they gave them in full tale to the king, that he might be the king's son in law. And Saul gave him Michal his daughter to wife" (1 Samuel 18:27).

Lama Sabachthani?

A Sermon Delivered On Lord's-day Morning,
March 2nd, 1890, Rev. C. H. SPURGEON,
At The Metropolitan Tabernacle, Newington

C. H. Spurgeon

"And about the ninth hour Jesus cried with a loud voice, saying, Eli, Eli, lama sabachthani? that is to say, My God, My God, why hast thou forsaken me?"— **Mat 27:46**

THERE WAS DARKNESS over all the land unto the ninth hour": this cry came out of that darkness. Expect not to see through its every word, as though it came from on high as a beam from the unclouded Sun of Righteousness. There is light in it, bright, flashing light: but there is a centre of impenetrable gloom, where the soul is ready to faint because of the terrible darkness.

Our Lord was then in the darkest part of his way. He had trodden the winepress now for hours, and the work was almost finished. He had reached the culminating point of his anguish. This is his dolorous lament from the lowest pit of misery—"My God, my God, why hast thou forsaken me?" I do not think that the records of time or even of eternity, contain a sentence more full of anguish. Here the wormwood and the gall, and all the other bitternesses, are outdone. Here you may look as into a vast abyss; and though you strain your eyes, and gaze till sight fails you, yet you perceive no bottom; it is measureless, unfathomable, inconceivable. This anguish of the Saviour on your behalf and mine is no more to be measured and weighed than the sin which needed it, or the love which endured it. We will adore where we cannot comprehend.

I have chosen this subject that it may help the children of God to understand a little of their infinite obligations to their redeeming Lord. You shall measure the height of his love, if it be ever mea-sured, by the depth of his grief, if that can ever be known. See with what a price he hath redeemed us from the curse of the law! As you see this, say to yourselves: What manner of people ought we to be! What measure of love ought we to return to one who bore the utmost penalty, that we might he delivered from the wrath to come? I do not profess that I can dive into this deep: I will only venture to the edge of the precipice, and bid you look down, and pray the Spirit of God to concentrate your mind upon this lamentation of our dying Lord, as it rises up through the thick darkness—"My God, my God, why hast thou forsaken me?

Our first subject of thought will be *the fact;* or, what he suffered—God had forsaken him. Secondly, we will note, *the enquiry;* or, why he suffered: this word "why" is the edge of the text. "Why hast thou forsaken me?" Then, thirdly, we will consider *the answer;* or, what came of his suffering. The answer flowed softly into the soul of the Lord Jesus without the need of words, for he ceased from his anguish with the triumphant shout of, "It is finished." His work was finished, and his bearing of desertion was a chief part of the work he had undertaken for our sake.

I. By the help of the Holy Spirit, let us first dwell upon THE FACT; or, what our Lord suffered. God had forsaken him. Grief of mind is harder to bear than pain of body. You can pluck up courage and endure the pang of sickness and pain, so long as the spirit is hale and brave; but if the soul itself be touched, and the mind becomes diseased with anguish, then every pain is increased in severity, and there is nothing with which to sustain it. Spiritual sorrows are the worst of mental miseries. A man may bear great depression of spirit about worldly matters, if he feels that he has his God to go to. He is cast down, but not in despair. Like David, he dialogues with himself, and he enquires, "Why art thou cast down, O my soul? and why art thou disquieted in me? Hope thou in God: for I shall yet praise him." But if the Lord be once withdrawn, if the comfortable light of his presence be shadowed even for an hour, there is a torment within the breast, which I can only liken to the prelude of hell. This is the greatest of all weights that can press upon the heart. This made the Psalmist plead, "Hide not thy face from me; put not thy servant away in anger." We can bear a bleeding body, and even a wounded spirit; but a soul conscious of desertion by God it beyond conception unendurable. When he holdeth back the face of his throne, and spreadeth his cloud upon it, who can endure the darkness?

This voice out of "the belly of hell" marks the lowest depth of the Saviour's grief. *The desertion was real.* Though under some aspects our Lord could say, "The Father is with me"; yet was it solemnly true that God did forsake him. It was not a failure of faith on his part which led him to imagine what was not actual fact. Our faith fails us, and then we think that God has forsaken us; but our Lord's faith did not for a moment falter, for he says twice, *"My* God, *my* God." Oh, the mighty double grip of his unhesitating faith! He seems to say, "Even if thou hast forsaken me, I have not forsaken thee." Faith triumphs, and there is no sign of any faintness of heart towards the living God. Yet, strong as is his faith, he feels that God has withdraw his comfortable fellowship, and he shivers under the terrible deprivation.

It was no fancy, or delirium of mind, caused by his weakness of body, the heat of the fever, the depression of his spirit, or the near approach of death. He was clear of mind even to this last. He bore up under pain, loss of blood, scorn, thirst, and desolation; making no complaint of the cross, the nails, and the scoffing. We read not in the Gospels of anything more than the natural cry of weakness, I thirst." All the tortures of his body he endured in silence; but when it came to being forsaken of God, then his great heart burst out into its "Lama sabachthani?" His one moan is concerning his God. It is not, "Why has Peter forsaken me? Why has Judas betrayed me?" These were sharp griefs, but this is the sharpest. This stroke has cut him to the quick: "My God, my God, why hast *thou* forsaken me?" It was no phantom of the gloom; it was a real absence which he mourned.

This was *a very remarkable desertion.* It is not the way of God to leave either his sons or his servants. His saints, when they come to die, in their great weakness and pain, find him near. They are made to sing because of the presence of God: "Yea, though I walk through the valley of the shadow of death, I will fear no evil: for thou art with me." Dying saints have clear visions of the living God. Our observation has taught us that if the Lord be away at other times, he is never absent from his people in the article of death, or in the fur-nace of affliction. Concerning the three holy children, we do not read that the Lord was ever visibly with them till they walked the fires of Nebuchadnezzar's furnace; but there and then the Lord met with them. Yes, beloved, it is God's use and wont to keep company with his afflicted people; and yet he forsook his Son in the hour of his tribulation! How usual it is to see the Lord with his faithful witnesses when resisting even unto blood! Read the Book of Martyrs, and I care not whether you study the former or the later persecutions, you will find them all lit up with the evident presence of the Lord with his witnesses. Did the Lord ever fail to support a martyr at the stake? Did he ever forsake one of his testifiers upon the scaffold? The testimony of the church has always been, that while the Lord has permitted his saints to suffer in body he has so divinely sustained their spirits that they have been more than conquerors, and have treated their sufferings as light afflictions. The fire has not been a "bed of roses," but it has been a chariot of victory. The sword is sharp, and death is bitter; but the love of Christ is sweet, and to die for him has been turned into glory. No, it is not God's way to forsake his champions, nor to leave even the least of his children in the trial hour.

As to our Lord, this forsaking was *singular.* Did his Father ever leave him before? Will you read the four Evangelists through and find any previous instance in which he complains of his Father for having forsaken him? No. He said, "I know that thou hearest me always." He lived in constant touch with God. His fellowship with the Father was always near and dear and clear; but now, for the first time, he cries, "why hast thou forsaken me?" It was very remark-able. It was a riddle only to be solved by the fact that he loved us and gave himself for us and in the execution of his loving purpose came even unto this sorrow, of mourning the absence of his God.

This forsaking was *very terrible*. Who can fully tell what it is to be forsaken of God? We can only form a guess by what we have our-selves felt under temporary and partial desertion. God has never left us, altogether; for he has expressly said, "I will never leave thee, nor forsake thee"; yet we have sometimes felt as if he had cast us off. We have cried, "Oh, that I know where I might find him!" The clear shinings of his love have been withdrawn. Thus we are able to form some little idea of how the Saviour felt when his God had for-saken him. The mind of Jesus was left to dwell upon one dark subject, and no cheering theme consoled him. It was the hour in which he was made to stand before God as consciously <u>the sin-bearer</u>, according to that ancient prophecy, "He shall bear their iniquities." Then was it true, "He hath made him to be sin for us." Peter puts it, "He his own self bare our sins in his own body on the tree." Sin, sin, sin was every where around and about Christ. He had no sin of his own; but the Lord had "laid on him the iniquity of us all." He had no strength given him from on high, no secret oil and wine poured into his wounds; but he was made to appear in the lone character of the Lamb of God, which taketh away the sin of the world; and therefore he must feel the weight of sin, and the turning away of that sacred face which cannot look thereon.

His Father, at that time, gave him no open acknowledgment. On certain other occasions a voice had been heard, saying, "This is my beloved Son, in whom I am well pleased"; but now, when such a testimony seemed most of all required, the oracle was dumb. He was hung up as an accursed thing upon the cross; for he was "made a curse for us, as it is written, Cursed is every one that hangeth on a tree"; and the Lord his God did not own him before men. If it had pleased the Father, he might have sent him twelve legions of angels; but not an angel came after the Christ had quitted Gethsemane. His despisers might spit in his face, but no swift seraph came to avenge the indignity. They might bind him, and scourge him, but none of all the heavenly host would interpose to screen his shoulders from the lash. They might fasten him to the tree with nails, and lift him up, and scoff at him; but no cohort of ministering spirits hastened to drive back the rabble, and release the Prince of life. No, he appeared to be forsaken, "smitten of God, and afflicted," delivered into the hands of cruel men, whose wicked hands worked him misery without stint. Well might he ask, "My God, my God, why hast thou forsaken me?"

But this was not all. His Father now dried up that sacred stream of peaceful communion and loving fellowship which had flowed hitherto throughout his whole earthly life. He said himself, as you remember, "Ye shall be scattered, every man to his own, and shall leave me alone: and yet I am not alone, because the Father is with me." Here was his constant comfort: but all comfort from this source was to be withdrawn. The divine Spirit did not minister to his human spirit. No communications with his Father's love poured into his heart. It was not possible that the Judge should smile upon one who repre-sented the prisoner at the bar. Our Lord's faith did not fail him, as I have already shown you, for he said, "My God, my God": yet no sen-sible supports were given to his heart, and no comforts were poured into his mind. One writer declares that Jesus did not taste of divine wrath, but only suffered a withdrawal of divine fellowship. What is the differ-ence? Whether God withdraw heat or create cold is all one. He was not smiled upon, nor allowed to feel that he was near to God; and this, to his tender spirit, was grief of the keenest order. A certain saint once said that in his sorrow he had from God "necessaries, but not suavities"; that which was meet, but not that which was sweet. Our Lord suffered to the extreme point of deprivation. He had not the light which makes existence to be life, and life to be a boon. You that know, in your degree, what it is to lose the conscious pre-sense and love of God, you can faintly guess what the sorrow of the Saviour was, now that he felt he had been forsaken of his God. "If the foundations be removed, what can the righteous do?" To our Lord, the Father's love was the foundation of everything; and when that was gone, all was gone. Nothing remained, within, without, above, when his own God, the God of his entire confidence, turned from him. Yes, God in very deed forsook our Saviour.

To be forsaken of God was *much more a source of anguish to Jesus than it would be to us.* "Oh," say you, "how is that?" I answer, because he was perfectly holy. A rupture between a perfectly holy being and the thrice holy God must be in the highest degree strange, abnormal, perplexing, and painful. If any man here, who is not at peace with God, could only know his true condition, he would swoon with fright. If you unforgiven ones only knew where you are, and what you are at this moment in the sight of God, you would never smile again till you were reconciled to him. Alas! we are insensible, hardened by the deceitfulness of sin, and therefore we do not feel our true condition. His perfect holiness made it to our Lord a dreadful calamity to be forsaken of the thrice holy God.

I remember, also, that our blessed Lord had lived in unbroken fellowship with God, and to be forsaken was a new grief to him. He had never known what the dark was till then: his life had been lived in the light of God. Think, dear child of God, if you had always dwelt in full communion with God, your days would have been as the days of heaven upon earth; and how cold it would strike to your heart to find yourself in the darkness of desertion. If you can conceive such a thing as happening to a perfect man, you can see why to our Well-beloved it was a special trial. Remember, he had enjoyed fellowship with God more richly, as well as more constantly, than any of us. His fellowship with the Father was of the highest, deepest, fullest order; and what must the loss of it have been? We lose but drops when we lose our joyful experience of heavenly fellowship; and yet the loss is killing: but to our Lord Jesus Christ the sea was dried up—I mean his sea of fellowship with the infinite God.

Do not forget that he was such a One that to him to be without God must have been an overwhelming calamity. In every part he was perfect, and in every part fitted for communion with God to a supreme degree. A sinful man has an awful need of God, but he does not know it; and therefore he does not feel that hunger and thirst after God which would come upon a perfect man could he be deprived of God. The very perfection of his nature renders it inevitable that the holy man must either be in communion with God, or be desolate. Imagine a stray angel! a seraph who has lost his God! Conceive him to be perfect in holiness, and yet to have fallen into a condition in which he cannot find his God! I cannot picture him; perhaps a Milton might have done so. He is sinless and trustful, and yet he has an overpowering feeling that God is absent from him. He has drifted into the nowhere—the unimaginable region behind the back of God. I think I hear the wailing of the cherub: "My God, my God, my God, where art thou?" What a sorrow for one of the sons of the morning! But here we have the lament of a Being far more capable of fellowship with the Godhead. In proportion as he is more fitted to receive the love of the great Father, in that proportion is his pining after it the more intense. As a Son, he is more able to commune with God than ever a servant-angel could be; and now that he is forsaken of God, the void within is the greater, and the anguish more bitter.

Our Lord's heart, and all his nature were, morally and spiritually, so delicately formed, so sensitive, so tender, that to be without God, was to him a grief which could not be weighed. I see him in the text bearing desertion, and yet I perceive that he cannot bear it. I know not how to express my meaning except by such a paradox. He cannot endure to be without God. He had surrendered himself to be left of God, as the representative of sinners must be, but his pure and holy nature, after three hours of silence, finds the position unendurable to love and purity; and breaking forth from it, now that the hour was over, he exclaims, "Why hast thou forsaken me?" He quarrels not with the suffering, but he cannot abide in the position which caused it. He seems as if he must end the ordeal, not because of the pain, but because of the moral shock. We have here the repetition after his passion of that loathing which he felt before it, when he cried, "If it be possible let this cup pass from me: nevertheless not as I will, but as thou wilt." "My God, my God, why hast thou forsaken me?" is the holiness of Christ amazed at the position of substitute for guilty men.

There, friends; I have done my best, but I seem to myself to have been prattling like a little child, talking about something infinitely above me. So I leave the solemn fact, that our Lord Jesus was on the tree forsaken of his God.

II. This brings us to consider THE ENQUIRY or, why he suffered.

Note carefully this cry—"My God, my God, why hast thou forsaken me?" It is pure anguish, undiluted agony, which crieth like this; but it is the agony of a godly soul; for only a man of that order would have used such an expression. Let us learn from it useful lessons. This cry is taken from "the Book." Does it not show our Lord's love of the sacred volume, that when he felt his sharpest grief, he turned to the Scripture to find a fit utterance for it? Here we have the opening sentence of the twenty-second Psalm. Oh, that we may so love the inspired Word that we may not only sing to its score, but even weep to its music!

Note, again, that our Lord's lament is an address to God. The godly, in their anguish, turn to the hand which smites them. The Saviour's outcry is not *against* God, but *to* God. "My God, my God": he makes a double effort to draw near. True Sonship is here. The child in the dark is crying after his Father—"My God, my God." Both the Bible and prayer were dear to Jesus in his agony.

Still, observe, it is a faith-cry; for though it asks, "Why hast thou forsaken me?" yet it first says, twice over, "My God, my God." The grip of appropriation is in the word "my"; but the reverence of humility is in the word "God." It is "'My *God*, my *God*,' thou art ever God to me, and I a poor creature. I do not quarrel with thee. Thy rights are unquestioned, for thou art my *God*. Thou canst do as thou wilt, and I yield to thy sacred sovereignty. I kiss the hand that smites me, and with all my heart

I cry, 'My God, my God.'" When you are delirious with pain, think of your Bible still: when your mind wanders, let it roam towards the mercy seat; and when your heart and your flesh fail, still live by faith, and still cry, "My God, my God."

Let us come close to the enquiry. It looked to me, at first sight, like *a question as of one distraught,* driven from the balance of his mind—not unreasonable, but too much reasoning, and therefore tossed about. "Why hast thou forsaken me?" Did not Jesus know? Did he not know why he was forsaken? He knew it most distinctly, and yet his manhood, while it was being crushed, pounded, dissolved, seemed as though it could not understand the reason for so great a grief. He must be forsaken; but could there be a sufficient cause for so sickening a sorrow? The cup must be bitter; but why this most nauseous of ingredients? I tremble lest I say what I ought not to say. I have said it, and I think there is truth—the Man of Sorrows was overborne with horror. At that moment the finite soul of the man Christ Jesus came into awful contact with the <u>infinite justice of God</u>. The one Mediator between God and man, the man Christ Jesus, beheld the holiness of God in arms against the sin of man, whose nature he had espoused. God was for him and with him in a certain unquestionable sense; but for the time, so far as his feeling went, God was against him, and necessarily withdrawn from him. It is not surprising that the holy soul of Christ should shudder at finding itself brought into painful contact with the <u>infinite justice of God</u>, even though its design was only to vindicate that justice, and glorify the Law-giver. Our Lord could now say, "All thy waves and thy billows are gone over me" and therefore he uses language which is all too hot with anguish to be dissected by the cold hand of a logical criticism. Grief has small regard for the laws of the grammarian. Even the holiest, when in extreme agony, though they cannot speak otherwise than according to purity and truth, yet use a language of their own, which only the ear of sympathy can fully receive. I see not all that is here, but what I can see I am not able to put in words for you.

I think I see, in the expression, submission and resolve. Our Lord does not draw back. There is a forward movement in the question: they who quit a business ask no more questions about it. He does not ask that the forsaking may end prematurely, he would only understand anew its meaning. He does not shrink, but the rather dedicates himself anew to God by the words, "My God, my God," and by seeking to review the ground and reason of that anguish which he is resolute to bear even to the bitter end. He would fain feel anew the motive which has sustained him, and must sustain him to the end. The cry sounds to me like deep submission and strong resolve, pleading with God.

Do you not think that *the amazement of our Lord, when he was "made sin for us"* (2Cr 5:21), led him thus to cry out? For such a sacred and pure being to be made a sin-offering was an amazing experience. Sin was laid on him, and he was treated as if he had been guilty, though he had personally never sinned; and now the infinite horror of rebellion against the most holy God fills his holy soul, the unrighteousness of sin breaks his heart, and he starts back from it, crying, "My God, my God, why hast thou forsaken *me?"* Why must I bear the dread result of contact I so much abhor?

Do you not see, moreover, *there was here a glance at his eternal purpose, and at his secret source of joy?* That "why" is the silver lining of the dark cloud, and our Lord looked wishfully at it. He knew that the desertion was needful it order that he might save the guilty, and he had an eye to that salvation as his comfort. He is not forsaken needlessly, nor without a worthy design. The design is in itself so dear to his heart that he yields to the passing evil, even though that evil be like death to him. He looks at that "why," and through that narrow window the light of heaven comes streaming into his darkened life.

"My God, my God, why hast thou forsaken me?" Surely our Lord dwelt on that "why," *that we might also turn our eyes that way.* He would have us see the why and the wherefore of his grief. He would have us mark the gracious motive for its endurance.

Think much of all your Lord suffered, but do not overlook the reason of it. If you cannot always understand how this or that grief worked toward the great end of the whole passion, yet believe that it has its share in the grand "why." Make a life-study of that bitter but blessed question, "Why hast thou forsaken me?" Thus the Saviour raises an inquiry not so much for himself as for us; and not so much because of any despair within his heart as because of a hope and a joy set before him, which were wells of comfort to him in his wilderness of woe.

Bethink you, for a moment, that the Lord God, in the broadest and most unreserved sense, could never, in very deed, have forsaken his most obedient Son. He was ever with him in the grand design of salvation. Towards the Lord Jesus, personally, God himself, personally, must ever have stood on terms of <u>infinite love.</u> Truly the Only Begotten was never more lovely to the Father than when he was obedient unto death, even the death of the cross! But we must look upon God here as the Judge of all the earth, and we must look upon the Lord Jesus also in his official capacity, as the Surety of the covenant, and the sacrifice for sin. The great Judge of all cannot smile upon him who has become the substitute for the guilty. Sin is loathed of God; and if, in order to its removal his own Son is made to bear it, yet, as sin, it is still loathsome, and he who bears it cannot be in happy communion with God. This was the dread necessity of expiation; but in the essence of things the love of the great Father to his Son never ceased, nor ever knew a diminution. Restrained in its flow it must be, but lessened at its fountain-head it could not be. Therefore, wonder not at the question, "Why hast thou forsaken me?"

III. Hoping to be guided by the Holy Spirit, I am coming to THE ANSWER, concerning which I can only use the few minutes which remain to me. "My God, my God, why hast thou forsaken me?" What is the outcome of this suffering? What was the reason for it? Our Saviour could answer his own question. If for a moment his manhood was perplexed, yet his mind soon came to clear apprehension; for he said, "It is finished"; and, as I have already said, he then referred to the work which in his lonely agony he had been performing. Why, then, did God forsake his Son? I cannot conceive any other answer than this— *he stood in our stead.* There was no reason in Christ why the Father should forsake him: he was perfect, and his life was without spot. God never acts without reason; and since there were no reasons in the character and person of the Lord Jesus why his Father should forsake him, we must look elsewhere. I do not know how others answer the question. I can only answer it in this one way.

> "Yet all the griefs he felt were ours,
> Ours were the woes he bore;
> Pangs, not his own, his spotless soul
> With bitter anguish tore.
> "We held him as condemn'd of heaven,
> An outcast from his God;
> While for our sins he groaned, he bled,
> Beneath his Father's rod."

He bore the sinner's sin, and he had to be treated, therefore, as though he were a sinner, though sinner be could never be. With his own full consent he suffered as though he had committed the transgressions which were laid on him. Our sin, and his taking it upon himself, is the answer to the question, "Why hast thou forsaken me?"

In this case we now see that *His obedience was perfect.* He came into the world to obey the Father, and he rendered that obedience to the very uttermost. The spirit of obedience could go no farther than for one who feels forsaken of God still to cling to him in solemn, avowed allegiance, still declaring before a mocking multitude his confidence in the afflicting God. It is noble to cry, "My God, my God," when one is asking, "Why hast thou forsaken me?" How much farther can obedience go? I see nothing beyond it. The soldier at the gate of Pompeii remaining at his post as sentry when the shower of burning ashes is falling, was not more true to his trust than he who adheres to a forsaking God with loyalty of hope.

Our Lord's suffering in this particular form was appropriate and necessary. It would not have sufficed for our Lord merely to have been pained in body, nor even to have been grieved in mind in other ways: he must suffer in this particular way. He must feel forsaken of God, because this is the necessary consequence of sin. For a man to be forsaken of God is the penalty which naturally and inevitably follows upon his breaking his relation with God. <u>What is death? What was the death that was threatened to Adam? "In the day that thou eatest thereof thou shalt surely die." Is death annihilation? Was Adam annihilated that day? Assuredly not: he lived many a year afterwards. But in the day in which he ate of the forbidden fruit he died, by being separated from God.</u> [Emphasis mine—Jim C.] The separation of the soul from God is spiritual death; just as the separation of the soul from the body is natural death. The sacrifice for sin must be put in the place of separation, and must bow to the penalty of death. By this placing of the Great Sacrifice under forsaking and death, it would be seen by all creatures throughout the universe that God could not have fellowship with sin. If even the Holy One, who stood the Just for the unjust, found God forsaking him, what must the doom of the actual sinner be! Sin is evidently always, in every case, a dividing influence, putting even the Christ himself, as a sin-bearer, in the place of distance.

This was necessary for another reason: there could have been no laying on of suffering for sin without the forsaking of the vicarious Sacrifice by the Lord God. So long as the smile of God rests on the man the law is not afflicting him. The approving look of the great Judge cannot fall upon a man who is viewed as standing in the place of the guilty. Christ not only suffered *from* sin, but *for* sin. If God will cheer and sustain him, he is not suffering for sin. The Judge is not inflicting suffering for sin if he is manifestly succouring the smitten one. There could have been no vicarious suffering on the part of Christ for human guilt, if he had continued consciously to enjoy the fall sunshine of the Father's presence. It was essential to being a victim in our place that he should cry, "My God, my God, why hast thou forsaken me?"

Beloved, see how marvellously, in the person of Christ, the Lord our God has vindicated his law! If to make his law glorious, he had said, "These multitudes of men have broken my law, and therefore they shall perish," the law would have been terribly magnified. But, instead thereof, he says, "Here is my Only Begotten Son, my other self; he takes on himself the nature of these rebellions creatures, and he consents that I should lay on him the load of their iniquity, and visit in his person the offences which might have been punished in the persons of all these multitudes of men: and I will have it so." When Jesus bows his head to the stroke of the law, when he submissively consents that his Father shall turn away his face from him, then myriads of worlds are astonished at the perfect holiness and stern justice of the Lawgiver. There are, probably, worlds innumerable throughout the boundless creation of God, and all these will see, in the death of God's dear Son, a declaration of his determination never to allow sin to be trifled with. If his own Son is brought before him, bearing the sin of others upon him, he will hide his face from him, as well as from the actually guilty. In God infinite love shines over all, but it does not eclipse his absolute justice any more than his justice is permitted to destroy his love. God hath all perfections in perfection, and in Christ Jesus we see the reflection of them. Beloved, this is a wonderful theme! Oh, that I had a tongue worthy of this subject! but who could ever reach the height of this great argument?

Once more, when enquiring, Why did Jesus suffer to be forsaken of the Father? we see the fact that *the Captain of our salvation was thus made perfect through suffering.* Every part of the road has been traversed by our Lord's own feet. Suppose, beloved, the Lord Jesus had never been thus forsaken, then one of his disciples might have been called to that sharp endurance, and the Lord Jesus could not have sympathized with him in it. He would turn to his Leader and Captain, and say to him, "Didst thou, my

Lord, ever feel this darkness?" Then the Lord Jesus would answer, "No. This is a descent such as I never made." What a dreadful lack would the tried one have felt! For the servant to bear a grief his Master never knew would be sad indeed. There would have been a wound for which there was no ointment, a pain for which there was no balm. But it is not so now. "In all their affliction he was afflicted." "He was in all points tempted like as we are, yet without sin." Wherein we greatly rejoice at this time, and so often as we are cast down. Underneath us is the deep experience of our forsaken Lord.

I have done when I have said three things. The first is, you and I that are believers in the Lord Jesus Christ and are resting in him alone for salvation, *let us lean hard,* let us bear with all our weight on our Lord. He will bear the full weight of all our sin and care. As to my sin, I hear its harsh accusings no more when I hear Jesus cry, "Why hast thou forsaken me?" I know that I deserve the deepest hell at the hand of God's vengeance; but I am not afraid. He will never forsake *me,* for he forsook his Son on my behalf. I shall not suffer for my sin, for Jesus has suffered to the full in my stead; yea, suffered so far as to cry, "My God, my God, why hast thou forsaken me?" Behind this brazen wall of substitution a sinner is safe. These "munitions of rock" guard all believers, and they may rest secure. The rock is cleft for me; I hide in its rifts, and no harm can reach me. You have a full atonement, a great sacrifice, a glorious vindication of the law; wherefore rest at peace, all you that put your trust in Jesus.

Next, if ever in our lives henceforth we should think that God hath deserted us, *let us learn from our Lord's example how to behave ourselves.* If God hath left thee, do not shut up thy Bible; nay, open it, as thy Lord did, and find a text that will suit thee. If God hath left thee, or thou thinkest so, do not give up prayer; nay, pray as thy Lord did, and be more earnest than ever. It thou thinkest God has forsaken thee, do not give up thy faith in him; but, like thy Lord, cry thou, "My God, my God," again and again. If thou hast had one anchor before, cast out two anchors now, and double the hold of thy faith. If thou canst not call Jehovah "Father," as was Christ's wont, yet call him thy "God." Let the personal pronouns take their hold—"My God, my God." Let nothing drive thee from thy faith. Still hold on Jesus, sink or swim. As for me, if ever I am lost, it shall be at the foot of the cross. To this pass have I come, that if I never see the face of God with acceptance, yet I will believe that he will be faithful to his Son, and true to the covenant sealed by oaths and blood. He that believeth in Jesus <u>hath everlasting life</u>: there I cling, like the limpet to the rock. There is but one gate of heaven; and even if I may not enter it, I will cling to the posts of its door. What am I saying? I shall enter in; for that gate was never shut against a soul that accepted Jesus; and Jesus saith, "Him that cometh to me I will in no wise cast out."

The last of the three points is this, *let us abhor the sin which brought such agony upon our beloved Lord.* What an accursed thing is sin, which crucified the Lord Jesus! Do you laugh at it? Will you go and spend an evening to see a mimic performance of it? Do you roll sin under your tongue as a sweet morsel, and then come to God's house, on the Lord's-day morning, and think to worship him? Worship him! Worship him, with sin indulged in your breast! Worship him, with sin loved and pampered in your life! O sirs, if I had a dear brother who had been murdered, what would you think of me if I valued the knife which had been crimsoned with his blood? —if I made a friend of the murderer, and daily consorted with the assassin, who drove the dagger into my brother's heart? Surely I, too, must be an accomplice in the crime! Sin murdered Christ; will you be a friend to it? Sin pierced the heart of the Incarnate God; can you love it? Oh, that there was an abyss as deep as Christ's misery, that I might at once hurl this dagger of sin into its depths, whence it might never be brought to light again! Begone, 0 sin! Thou art banished from the heart where Jesus reigns! Begone, for thou hast crucified my Lord, and made him cry, "Why hast thou forsaken me?" O my hearers, if you did but know yourselves, and know the love of Christ, you would each one vow that you would harbour sin no longer. You would be indignant at sin, and cry,

"The dearest idol I have known,
Whate'er that idol be,
Lord, I will tear it from its throne,
And worship only thee,"

May that be the issue of my morning's discourse, and then I shall
be well content. The Lord bless you! May the Christ who
suffered for you, bless you, and out of his darkness may your
light arise! Amen.

Psychopannychia

OR, A REFUTATION OF THE ERROR ENTERTAINED
BY SOME UNSKILFUL PERSONS, WHO IGNORANTLY
IMAGINE THAT IN THE INTERVAL BETWEEN DEATH
AND THE JUDGMENT THE SOUL SLEEPS. TOGETHER
WITH AN EXPLANATION OF THE CONDITION AND
LIFE OF THE SOUL AFTER THIS PRESENT LIFE.

John Calvin

TRANSLATOR'S NOTE FOR PSYCHOPANNYCHIA; OR, THE SOUL'S IMAGINARY SLEEP.

The title of PSYCHOPANNYCHIA derived from Greek words which signify "the sleep of the soul;" the object of the Tract being to show, partly from reason, but more especially from Scripture, that there is no such sleep. It was published in 1534, when CALVIN was twenty-five years of age, and is, consequently, with the exception of the Commentary on the Clementia of Seneca, published in 1532, the earliest of all his writings, and two years earlier than the Institutes, the first known edition of which appeared in 1536. It thus possesses, especially to those who delight to trace the progress of a master mind, an interest additional to that which its merit gives it.

The figment which it refutes is said by CALVIN to be of Arabian origin, but was first brought prominently into notice by some of the wildest fanatics among the ANABAPTISTS, for whom everything new and monstrous appears to have had an irresistible attraction. In more modern times, attempts have been made to give it a philosophical shape, as a necessary corollary from the dogma of Materialism advocated by Priestley and others.

It would seem that the figment, wild and irrational though it is, had made considerable progress at an early period of the Reformation, and counted numerous converts, not merely among the fanatics who had revived it, but in more respectable quarters, where better things might have been expected.

One is puzzled to understand why it should have been received with so much favor; for the idea which it suggests, so far from being attractive, is naturally revolting. It was probably welcomed, not so much for its own sake, as for the great assistance which it was supposed capable of giving in THE

POPISH CONTROVERSY. Were it once established that the soul falls asleep at death, and will not awake to consciousness till again united to the body at the resurrection, THE POPE would forthwith be excluded from the larger half of his domain, and deprived of the most lucrative branches of his trade! There would neither be SAINTS to whom divine honors could be paid, nor PURGATORY out of which poor souls might be delivered with more or less expedition, according to the number of well-paid masses that were said for them!

If the cordial reception given to the dogma was owing to the collateral benefit thus supposed to be derived from it, it only adds another to the many instances in which blind man would arrogantly give lessons to his Maker, and arrange the world on a better plan than His infinite wisdom has devised. Because it would furnish a triumphant refutation of Popish legends and fictions — the soul must be made to perish with the body, and a common ruin overtake both!

It would appear that the subject had attracted attention in England, for we find that the TRACT was translated in the reign of Queen Elizabeth. The title-page is as follows: — "A Treatise of the Immortality of the Soul, by which it is proved that souls after the departure of the bodies are awake and do live: against those that think they do sleep. By JOHN CALVIN. Translated out of French by Tho. Stocker." It was "Imprinted by John Day. London, 1581."

In the PSYCHOPANNYCHIA, CALVIN, knowing the kind of people he had to deal with, accommodates himself to their capacities; and instead of entering largely into speculative disquisitions which the subject seems to suggest, and to which the metaphysical cast of his own mind must have strongly inclined him, dwells chiefly on THE SCRIPTURAL ARGUMENT — carefully examining all the passages which the advocates of the dogma had adduced as favorable to their view, and adducing others by which it is completely overthrown. If by the adoption of this plan, the TRACT loses somewhat in point of philosophical exactness, it gains much in richness of scriptural illustration; and proves that, even at this early period, in writing his first theological publication, CALVIN gave promise of the almost unrivaled excellence to which he ultimately trained as a COMMENTATOR.

Henry Beveridge

May 1851.

PREFACE BY JOHN CALVIN TO A FRIEND.

LONG ago, when certain pious persons invited, and even urged me, to publish something for the purpose of repressing the extravagance of those who, alike ignorantly and tumultuously, maintain that THE SOUL DIES OR SLEEPS, I could not be induced by all their urgency, so averse did I feel to engage in that kind of dispute. At that time, indeed, I was not without excuse, partly because I hoped that that absurd dogma would soon vanish of its own accord, or at least be confined to a few triflers; partly because I did not think it expedient to engage with a party whose camp and weapons and stratagems I was scarcely acquainted with. For, as yet, nothing had reached me except murmurs and hoarse sounds, so that, to engage with those who had not yet come forth into the arena, seemed to be nothing better than blindly striking the air. The result, however, has been different from what I hoped. These babblers have so actively exerted themselves, that they have already drawn thousands into their insanity. And even the error itself has, I see, been aggravated. At first, some only vaguely alleged THAT THE SOUL SLEEPS, without defining what they wished to be understood by "sleep." Afterwards arose those yucokonoi, who murder Souls, though without inflicting a wound. The error of the former, indeed, was not to be borne; but I think that the madness of the latter ought to be severely repressed. Both are unsupported by reason and judgment; but it is not so easy to persuade others of this without openly refuting their vanity, and exposing it, so to speak, to their face. This is only to be done by exhibiting it as it appears in their writings. They are said to circulate their follies in a kind of Tracts, which I have never happened to see. I have only received some notes from a friend, who had taken down what he had cursorily heard from their lips, or collected by some other means.

Although one reason for my not writing has been partially removed by these notes, the other still remains. However, while the men by whispers, and a garrulity for which they are remarkable, stealthily insinuate themselves, and ensnare no fewer in their error than the circulation of printed books could enable them to do, I feel that I could not well defend myself from the charge of being a traitor to the Truth were I, in such urgent circumstances, to keep back and remain silent! And, while I trust that my labor will be of the greatest use to the more unskillful and less experienced, and not without some use also to the moderately instructed who have given some slight attention to the subject, I will not hesitate to give a reason of my faith to all the good — not such a reason, perhaps, as may fully equip them both for defense and for carrying the war into the enemies' camp, but such a one as will not leave them altogether unarmed. Had the importunity of these men in circulating their dreams among the vulgar allowed me, I would willingly have declined a contest of this nature, in which the fruit gained is not equal to the labor expended, this being one of the cases to which the Apostle's exhortation to be soberly wise particularly applies. But though we long for this soberness, they will not allow us to employ it. Still, my endeavor will be to treat the subject with moderation, and keep it within due bounds.

I wish some other method of cutting away the evil, which makes far too much progress, had been devised, so as to prevent it from gaining ground daily, and eating in like a cancer. Nor does it now appear for the first time; for we read that it originated with some Arabs, who maintained that "The soul dies with the body, and that both rise again at the Day of Judgment." (Euseb. Eccl. Hist. lib. 6 c. 36; Aug. lib. de Haeres. c. 83, dist. 16; John 2:) Some time after, John, Bishop of Rome, broached it, and was forced to recant by the Theological Faculty of Paris. (Gerson in Sermone Pasch. priore.) It lay smoldering for some ages, but has lately begun to send forth sparks, being stirred up by some dregs of Anabaptists. These, spread abroad far and wide, have kindled torches — and would that they were soon extinguished by that voluntary rain which the Lord hath set apart for his inheritance!

I will plead the cause without hatred to any man, without personal affront to any man, in short, without any bitterness of invective, so that no one shall be able to complain of being hurt, or even slightly offended. And yet, in the present day, persons may be seen giving full scope to a carping, biting, scoffing temper, who, if you were only to lay a finger on them, would make a lamentable outcry that "the Unity of the Church is rent in pieces, and Charity violated!" To such let this be our answer: *First,* That we acknowledge no Unity except in Christ; no Charity of which He is not the bond; and that, therefore, the chief point in preserving Charity is to maintain Faith sacred and entire. *Secondly,* That this Discussion may proceed without any violation of charity, provided the ears with which they listen correspond with the tongue which I employ.

To you, Honored Sir, I have, thought it right to dedicate this small Tract on many accounts, but on one account especially, — because I see that, amid those tumults of vain opinions with which giddy spirits disturb the peace of the Church, you stand firm and complete in prudence and. moderation.

ORLEANS, 1534.

TO THE READER.

ON again reading this DISCUSSION, I observe that, in the heat of argument, some rather severe and harsh expressions have escaped me, which may, perhaps, give offense to delicate ears; and as I know that there are some good men into whose minds some part of this dogma has been instilled, either from excessive credulity or ignorance of Scripture, with which at the time they were not armed so as to be able to resist, I am unwilling to give them offense so far as they will allow me, since they are neither perverse nor malicious in their error. I wish, therefore, to warn such beforehand not to take anything said as an affront to themselves, but to understand that, whenever I use some freedom of speech, I am referring to the nefarious herd of Anabaptists, from whose fountain this noxious stream did, as I observed, first flow, and against whom nothing I have said equals their deserts. If I am to have a future fight with them, I am determined they shall find me, if not a very skillful, yet certainly a firm, and as I dare promise, by God's grace, an invincible defender of the Truth. And yet against them I have not given immoderate vent to my bile, having constantly refrained from all pertness and petulance of speech; tempering my pen so as to be fitter for teaching than forcing, and yet able to draw such as are unwilling to be led. It was certainly much more my intention to bring all back into the right way, than to provoke them to anger.

All who are to read I exhort and beseech by the Name of God, and of our Lord Jesus Christ, that they bring an impartial judgment and a mind prepared as it were to be the seat of truth. I am aware of the power which novelty has to tickle the ears of certain persons: but we ought to reflect that "Truth has only one voice" — that which proceeds from the lips of our Lord. To

Him alone ought we to open our ears when the doctrine of Salvation is in question, while to all others we should keep them shut. His word, I say, is not new, but that which was from the beginning, is, and always shall be. And as those err who, when the word of God, which had been laid aside through perverse custom or sloth, is brought to light, charge it with novelty; so they err, in the other direction, who are like reeds driven by the wind, nay, nod and bend at the slightest breeze! When we speak of learning Christ, do we mean that we are to lend an ear, without regard to the word of God, to any doctrine even though true? If you receive it as from man, will you not embrace falsehood with the same facility? For what has man of his own save vanity?

Such was not the conduct of those who, when they had received the word, searched the Scriptures to see whether these things were so (Acts 17:11) — a noble example, if we would imitate it; but we, I know not from what sloth, or rather contempt, receive the word of God in such a way that when we have learned three syllables, we immediately swell up with an opinion of wisdom, and think ourselves rich men and kings! Hence, you see so many who, unlearned themselves, keep tragically bawling out about the ignorance of the age! But what can you do? They are called, and would wish to be thought Christians, because they have got a slight knowledge of some commonplaces; and as they would be ashamed to be ignorant of anything, they with the greatest confidence, as if from a tripod, give forth decisions upon all things. Hence so many schisms, so many errors, so many stumbling blocks to our faith, through which the name and word of God are blasphemed among the ungodly. At length, (this is the head of the evil!) while they proceed obstinately to defend whatever they have once rashly babbled, they begin to consult the oracles of God, in order that they may there find support to their errors. Then, good God! what do they not pervert, what do they not adulterate and corrupt, that they may, I do not say bend, but distort it to their own view? As was truly said by the poet, "Fury supplies armor."

Is this the way of learning — to roll the Scriptures over and over, and twist them about in search of something that may minister to our lust, or to force them into subjection to our sense? Nothing can be more absurd than this, O pernicious pest! O tares certainly sown by an enemy's hand, for the purpose of rendering the true seed useless! And do we still wonder at the many sects among those who had at first given in their adherence to the gospel and the reviving word? I, for my part, am terrified by the dreadful denunciation,

"The kingdom of God shall be taken from you, and given to a nation bringing forth the fruits thereof." (Matthew 21:43.)

Here, however, I desist from my complaints: for I should write a large volume were I to declaim in just terms on the perversity of this age. Let us, brethren, warned by so many examples, at length, though late, become wise. Let us always hang on our Lord's lips, and neither add to His wisdom nor mix up with it anything of our own, lest like leaven it corrupt the whole mass, and make even the very salt which is within us to be without savor. Let us show ourselves to be such disciples as our Lord wishes to have — poor, empty, and void of self-wisdom: eager to learn but knowing nothing, and even wishing to know nothing but what He has taught; shunning everything of foreign growth as the deadliest poison.

I would here obviate the objections of those who will blame my present undertaking, charging me with stirring up fierce contests about nothing, and making trifling differences the source of violent dissensions: for there are not wanting some who so reproach me. My answer is, that when Divine Truth is avowedly attacked, we must not tolerate the adulteration of one single *iota* of it. It is certainly no trivial matter to see God's light extinguished by the devil's darkness; and besides, this matter is of greater moment than many suppose. Nor is it true as they allege that he who does not acquiesce in the errors of others, shows deadly hate by dissenting from them. I have censured the curiosity of those who would agitate questions which are truly nothing else than mere tortures to the intellect. But after they have stirred this *camarina,* their temerity must be repressed, lest it should prevail over the truth. Whether I have succeeded in this I know not: it was certainly my wish, and I have done the best I could. If others can do better, let them come forward for the public good!

BASEL, 1536.

PSYCHOPANNYCHIA.

IN following out this Discussion, I will not labor the matter much, but endeavor to explain myself with the greatest simplicity and clearness. In every Discussion, indeed, it is of the greatest consequence that the subject be clearly seen by the writer, and laid distinctly before his readers; lest either he wander beyond his bounds, and lose himself in mere loquacity, or they, ignorant of the ground, go astray from not knowing the road. This is particularly necessary to be observed when the subject is matter of controversy, since there we do not merely propose to teach, but have to do with an opponent who (such is man's temper) certainly will not, if he can help it, allow himself to be vanquished, nor will confess defeat so long as he can sport and make a diversion by cavilling rejoinders and tergiversation. The best method of pressing an enemy and holding him fast so that he cannot escape, is to exhibit the controverted point, and explain it so distinctly and clearly, that you can bring him at once as it were to close quarters.

Our controversy, then, relapses to The Human Soul. Some, while admitting it to have a real existence, imagine that it sleeps in a state of insensibility from Death to The Judgment-day, when it will awake from its sleep; while others will sooner admit anything than its real existence, maintaining that it is merely a vital power which is derived from arterial spirit on the action of the lungs, and being unable to exist without body, perishes along with the body, and vanishes away and becomes evanescent till the period when the whole man shall be raised again. We, on the other hand, maintain both that it is a substance, and after the death of the body truly lives, being endued both with sense and understanding. Both these points we undertake to prove by clear passages of Scripture. Here let human wisdom give place; for though it thinks much about the soul it perceives no certainty with regard to it. Here, too, let Philosophers give place, since on almost all subjects their regular practice is to put neither end nor measure to their dissensions, while on this subject in particular they quarrel, so that you will scarcely find two of them agreed on any single point! Plato, in some passages, talks nobly of the faculties of the soul; and Aristotle, in discoursing of it, has surpassed all in acuteness. But what the soul is, and whence it is, it is vain to ask at them, or indeed at the whole body of Sages, though they certainly thought more purely and wisely on the subject than some amongst ourselves, who boast that they are the disciples of Christ.

But before proceeding farther, we must cut off all handle for logomachy, which might be furnished by our giving the name of "soul" and "spirit" indiscriminately to that which is the subject of controversy, and yet sometimes speaking of the two as different. By Scripture usage different meanings are given to these terms; and most people, without attending to this difference, take up the first meaning which occurs to them, keep fast hold of it, and pertinaciously maintain it. Others, having seen "soul" sometimes used for "life," hold this to be invariably the case, and will not allow themselves to be convinced of the contrary. If met with the passage from David,

"Their soul will be blessed in life," (Psalm 49:19)

they will interpret, that their life is blessed in life. In like manner, if the passage from Samuel be produced, "By thy life, and by thy soul's life," (2 Samuel 11:11,) they will say, that there is no meaning in these terms. We know that "soul" is very often used for *life* in such passages as the following, "My soul is in my hands," — "Why do I tear my flesh with my teeth, and carry my soul in my hands?" — "Is not the soul more than meat," — "Thou fool, this night shall thy soul be required of thee." (Psalm 119:109; Job 13:14; Matthew 6:25; Luke 12:20.) There are other similar passages which these soulslayers always have in their mouth. There is no ground, however, for their great self-complacency, since they ought to observe that *soul* is there used metonymically for *life,* because the soul is the cause of life, and life depends on the soul — a figure which boys learn even from their rudiments. It is impossible not to wonder at the presumption of these men, who have so high an opinion of themselves, and would fain be thought wise by others, though they require to be taught the use of figures and the first elements of speech. In this sense it was said that "the soul of Jonathan was knit to the soul of David" — the soul of Sychem (Shechem) "clave unto Dinah the daughter of Jacob;" and Luke says, that "the multitude of the believers was of one heart and soul." (1 Samuel 18:1; Genesis 34:3; Acts 4:32.) Who sees not that there is much force in such Hebraisms as the following? "Bless the Lord, O my soul," — "My soul doth magnify the Lord," — "Say to my soul, I am thy salvation." (Psalm 103:1; 104:1; Luke 1:46.) An indescribable something more is expressed than if it were said without addition, Bless the Lord; I magnify the Lord, Say to me, I am thy salvation!

Sometimes the word "soul" is used merely for a *living man,* as when sixty souls are said to have gone down into Egypt.. (Exodus 1:5.) Again, "The soul that sinneth, it shall die," — "The soul which turneth aside to wizards and soothsayers shall die the death," etc. (Ezekiel 28:4; Leviticus 20:6.) Sometimes also it is called the *breath* which men inhale and respire, and in which the vital motion of the body resides. In this sense I understand the following passages, "Anxiety seizes me though my whole soul is still in me,"— "His soul is in him," — "Let the soul of the child return within him." (2 Samuel 1:9; Acts 20:10; 1 Kings 17:21.) Nay, in the very same sense in which we say, in ordinary language, that the soul is "breathed out" and "expires," Scripture speaks of the soul "departing," as when it is said of Rachel, "And when her soul was departing (for she died) she called the name of the child Benoni" (Genesis 35:18.)

We know that spirit is *literally* "breath" and "wind," and for this reason is frequently called pnoh<n by the Greeks. We know that it is used by Isaiah for a thing vain and worthless, "We have conceived and brought forth spirit," or "wind." (Isaiah 26:18.) It is very often taken for what is *regenerated* in us by the Spirit of God. For when Paul says that "the spirit lusteth against the flesh," (Galatians 5:17,) he does not mean that the soul fights with the flesh, or reason with desire; but that the soul itself, in as far as it is governed by the Spirit of God, wrestles with itself, though in as far as it is still devoid of the Spirit of God, it is subject to its lusts. We know that when the two terms are joined, "soul" means *will,* and "spirit" means *intellect.* Isaiah thus speaks,

"My soul hath longed for thee in the night, but I will also wake to thee in my spirit, within me" (Isaiah 26:9.)

And when Paul prays that the Thessalonians may be entire in spirit, and soul, and body, so that they may be without blame at the coming of Jesus Christ, (1 Thessalonians 5:23,) his meaning is, that they may think and will all things rightly, and may not use their members as instruments of unrighteousness. To the same effect the Apostle elsewhere says, that the word of God is quick and piercing, like a two-edged sword, reaching to the division of soul and spirit, of the joints and marrow, and is a discerner of the thoughts of the heart. (Hebrews 4:12.) In this last passage, however, some understand by "spirit" that reasoning and willing essence of which we now dispute; and by "soul," the vital motion and senses which philosophers call superior and inferior, i.e., ojrmai< kai< aijsqh>seiv. But since in numerous passages both parties hold it to mean the immortal essence which is the cause of life in man, let them not raise disputes about mere names, but attend to the thing itself, by whatever name distinguished. How real it is let us now show.

And we will begin with man's creation, wherein we shall see of what nature he was made at first. The Sacred History tells us (Genesis 1:26) of the purpose of God, before man was created, to make him "*after his own image and likeness.*" These expressions cannot possibly be understood of his body, in which, though the wonderful work of God appears more than in all other creatures, his image nowhere shines forth. (Ambros. lib. 6, hex. August. cap. 4: de Trinit. et alibi.) For who is it that speaks thus, "Let us make man in our own image and likeness?" God himself, who is a Spirit, and cannot be represented by any bodily shape. But as a bodily image, which exhibits the external face, ought to express to the life all the traits and features, that thus the statue or picture may give an idea of all that may be seen in the original, so this image of God must, by its likeness, implant some knowledge of God in our minds. I hear that some triflers say that the image of God refers to the dominion which was given to man over the brutes, and that in this respect man has some resemblance to God, whose dominion is over all. Into this mistake even Chrysostom fell when he was carried away in the heat of debate against the insane Anthropomorphites. But Scripture does not allow its meaning to be thus evaded: for Moses, to prevent any one from placing this image in the flesh of man, first narrates that the body was formed out of clay, and makes no mention of the image of God; thereafter, he says, that "the breath of life" was; introduced into this clay body, making the image of God not to become effulgent in man till he was complete in all his parts. What then, it will be asked, do you think that that breath of life is the image of God? No, indeed, although I might say so with many, and perhaps not improperly. (Hilar. in Psalm 63; Aug. Lib. de Spiritu et Anima, cap. 39; Basil, hex. Hem. 8.) For what if I should maintain that the distinction was constituted by the word of God, by which that breath of life is distinguished from the souls of brutes? For whence do the souls of other animals arise? God says, "Let the earth bring forth the living soul," etc. Let that which has sprung of earth be resolved into earth. But the soul of man is not of the earth. It was made by the mouth of the Lord, i.e., by his secret power.

Here, however, I do not insist, lest it should become a ground of quarrel. All I wish to obtain is, that the image itself is separate from the flesh. Were it otherwise, there would be no great distinctions, in man from its being said that he was made *in the image of God;* and yet it is repeatedly brought forward in Scripture, and highly celebrated. For what occasion was there to introduce God as deliberating, and, as it were, making it a subject of consultation, whether he should make an ordinary creature? In regard to all these things, "He spake, and it was done." When he comes to this image, as if he were about to give a singular manifestation, he calls in his wisdom and power, and meditates with himself before he puts his hand to the work. Were these figurative modes of expression which represent the Lord, ajnqrwpopaqw~v, (in a human manner,) in adaptation to our feeble capacity, so anxiously employed by Moses for a thing of nought? Was it not rather to give an exalted idea of the image of God impressed on man? Not contented with saying it once, he repeats it again and again. Whatever philosophers or these dreamers may pretend, we hold that nothing can bear the image of God but spirit, since God is a Spirit.

Here we are not left to conjecture what resemblance this image bears to its archetype. We easily learn it from the Apostle. (Colossians 3:10.) When he enjoins us to "put on the new man, which is renewed in knowledge after the image of him who created him," he clearly shows what this image is, or wherein it consists; as he also does when he says, (Ephesians 4:24,) "Put on the new man, who has been created after God in knowledge and true holiness." When we would comprehend all these things, in one word we say, that man, in respect of spirit, was made partaker of the wisdom, justice, and goodness of God. This mode of expression was followed by two sacred writers. The one, in dividing man into two parts — *body*, taken from the earth, and *soul*, derived from the image of God — briefly comprehended what Moses had more fully expressed, (Ecclesiastes 17:1,) "God created man, and made him after his own image." The other, desiring to state exegetically how far the image of God extended, called man "inexterminable," because created in the image of God. (Wisdom 2:23.) I would not urge the authority of these writers strongly on our opponents, did they not allege them against us. Still they ought to have some weight, if not as canonical, at least as ancient pious writers strongly supported. But, leaving them, let us hold the image of God in man to be that which can only have its seat in the Spirit.

Let us now hear what *Scripture* more distinctly states concerning the Soul. When Peter speaks of the salvation of the soul, and says that carnal lusts war against the soul; when he enjoins us to keep our souls chaste, and calls Christ the "Bishop of our souls," (1 Peter 1:9, 22; 2 Peter 2:25,) what could he mean but that there were souls which could be saved — which could be assailed by vicious desires — which could be kept chaste, and be ruled by Christ their Bishop? In the history of Job we read, (Job 4:19,) How much more those who dwell in houses of clay, and have a foundation of earth?" This, if you attend to it, you must see to apply to the soul, which dwells in a clay body. He did not call man a vessel of clay, but says that he inhabits a vessel of clay, as if the good part of man (which is the soul) were contained in that earthly abode. Thus Peter says, (1 Peter 1:13,) "I think it right, as long as I am in this tabernacle, to stir you up by way of remembrance, knowing that in a short time I must put off this my tabernacle." By this form of expression we might, if we are not very stupid, understand that there is something in a tabernacle, and something which is taken out of a tabernacle, or which, as he says, is to put off a tabernacle. The same manifest distinction between the flesh and the spirit is made by the author of the Epistle to the Hebrews, (Hebrews 12:9,) when he calls those by whom we were begotten the parents of one flesh; but says that there is one God, "the Father of spirits." Shortly after, having called God the King of the heavenly Jerusalem, he subjoins that its citizens are angels and

"the spirits of just men made perfect." (Hebrews 12:23.)

Nor do I see how we can otherwise understand Paul, when he says, (2 Corinthians 7:1,) "Having, therefore, these promises, let us cleanse ourselves from all pollution of the flesh and spirit." For it is clear that he does not there make the comparison which he elsewhere frequently uses when he attributes defilement to the spirit, by which term, in other passages: he merely means purity.

I will add another passage, though I see that those who wish to cavil will immediately betake themselves to their glosses. The passage is, (1 Corinthians 2:11,) "Who of men knows the things of a man, save the spirit of man that is in him? so also no man knows the things of God, but the Spirit of God." He might have said, that man knows the things which are his; but he applied the name to that part in which the power of thinking and understanding resides. Also, when he said, (Romans 8:16,) "The Spirit of God bears witness with our spirit, that we are the sons of God," did he not use the same peculiarity of expression? But, might we not convince them by a single passage? We know how often our Savior condemned the error of the Sadducees, which partly consisted, as Luke states in the Acts, (Acts 23:8,) in denying the existence of spirit, The words are, "The Sadducees say that there is no resurrection, neither angel nor spirit; but the Pharisees acknowledge all these." I fear they will cavil, and say that the words must be understood of the Holy Spirit or of angels. But this objection is easily met. He both mentioned the angels separately; and it is certain that those Pharisees had no knowledge of the Holy Spirit. This will be still better understood by those who know Greek. Luke uses the term pneu~ma without adding the article, which he certainly would have added had he been speaking of the Holy Spirit.

If this does not stop their mouths, I do not see by what argument they can either be led or drawn, unless they choose to say that the opinion of the Sadducees, in denying spirit, was not condemned, or that of the Pharisees, in asserting it, approved. This quibble is met by the very words of the Evangelist: for, after stating Paul's confession, "I am a Pharisee," he adds this opinion held by the Pharisees. We must therefore either say that Paul used a *crafty* and malicious *pretence,* (this could not be, in a confession of faith!) or that he held with the Pharisees on the subject of spirit. But if we give credit to *History,* (Eccl. Hist., c. 4: cap. 13,) this belief among the Apostles was as firm and certain as that of The Resurrection of the Dead, or any other leading article of our faith. It will not be out of place here to quote the words, of Polycarp, a man breathing the spirit of a martyr in all his words and actions, (Hist. Eccl., cap. 19,) one who was a disciple of the Apostles, and so purely delivered what he heard from them to posterity, that he never allowed it to be in any degree adulterated. He, then, among many illustrious sayings which he uttered when brought to the stake, said, that on that day he was to appear before God in spirit. About the same time Melito, Bishop of Sardis, (Hist. Eccl., c. 24,) a man of like integrity, wrote a treatise, On Body and Soul. Were it now extant, our present labor would be superfluous: and so much did this belief prevail in a better age, that Tertullian places it among the common and primary conceptions of the mind which are commonly apprehended by nature. (Tertull. de Resurrect. Carnis.)

Although several arguments have already been advanced which, if I mistake not, establish the point for which I contend, viz., That the spirit or soul of man is a substance distinct from the body, what is now to be added will make the point still more certain. For I come to *The Second Head,* which I propose to discuss, viz., THAT THE SOUL, AFTER THE DEATH OF THE BODY, STILL SURVIVES, ENDUED WITH SENSE AND INTELLECT. And it is a mistake to suppose that I am here affirming anything else than THE IMMORTALITY OF THE SOUL. For those who admit that the soul lives, and yet deprive it of all sense, feign a soul which has none of the properties of soul, or dissever the soul from itself, seeing that its nature, without which it cannot possibly exist, is to move, to feel, to be vigorous, to understand. As Tertullian says, "The soul of the soul is perception." (Lib. de Carne Christi.)

Let us now learn this IMMORTALITY from Scripture. When Christ exhorts his followers not to fear those who can kill the body, but cannot kill the soul, but to fear him who, after he hath killed the body, is able to cast the soul into the fire of Gehenna, (Matthew 10:28,) does he not intimate that the soul survives death? Graciously, therefore, has the Lord acted towards us, in not leaving our souls to the disposal of those who make no scruple of butchering them, or at least attempt it, but without the ability to do so. Tyrants torture, maim, burn, scourge., and hang, but it is only the body! It is God alone who has power over the soul, and can send it into hell fire. Either, therefore, the soul survives the body, or it is false to say that tyrants have no power over the soul! I hear them reply, that the soul is indeed slain for the present when death is inflicted, but does not perish, inasmuch as it will be raised again. When they would escape in this way, they must grant that neither is the body slain, since it too will rise; and because both are preserved against the day of judgment, neither perishes! But the words of Christ admit that the body is killed, and testify at the same time that the soul is safe. This form of expression Christ uses when he says, (John 2:19,) "Destroy this temple, and in three days I will raise it up." He was speaking of the temple of his body. In like manner he exempts it from their power, when, in dying, he commends it into his Father's hands, as Luke writes, and David had foretold. (Luke 23:4,6; Psalm 31:6.) And Stephen, after his example, says "Lord Jesus, receive my spirit!" (Acts 7:59.) Here they absurdly pretend that Christ commends his life to his Father, and Stephen his to Christ, to be kept against the day of Resurrection. But the words, especially those of Stephen, imply something very different from this. And the Evangelist adds, concerning Christ, that having bowed his head, he delivered his spirit. (John 19:30.) These words cannot refer to panting or action of the lungs.

Not less evidently does the Apostle Peter show that, After death, the soul both exists and lives, when he says (1 Peter 1:19) that Christ preached to the spirits in prison, not merely forgiveness for salvation to the spirits of the righteous, but also confusion to the spirits of the wicked. For so I interpret the passage, which has puzzled many minds; and I am confident that, under favorable auspices, I will make good my interpretation. For after he had spoken of the humiliation of the cross of Christ, and shown that all the righteous must be conformed to his image, he immediately thereafter, to prevent them from falling into despair, makes mention of the Resurrection, to teach them how their tribulations were to end.

For he states that Christ did not fall under death, but, subduing it, came forth victorious. He indeed says in words, that he was

"put to death in the flesh, but quickened by the Spirit," (1 Peter 3:18)

but just in the same sense in which Paul says that he suffered in the humiliation of the flesh, but was raised by the power of the Spirit. Now, in order that believers might understand that the power belongs to them also, he subjoins that Christ exerted this power in regard to others, and not only towards the living, but also towards the dead; and, moreover, not only towards his servants, but also towards unbelievers and the despisers of his grace.

Let us understand, moreover, that the sentence is defective, and wants one of its two members. Many examples of this occur in Scripture, especially when, as here, several sentiments are comprehended in one clause. And let no one wonder that the holy Patriarchs who waited for the redemption of Christ are shut up in prison. As they saw the light at a distance, under a cloud and shade, (as those who see the feeble light of dawn or twilight,) and had not yet an exhibition of the divine blessing in which they rested, he gave the name of prison to their expectancy.

The meaning of the Apostle will therefore be, that Christ in spirit preached to those other spirits who were in prison — in other words, that the virtue of the redemption obtained by Christ appeared and was exhibited to the spirits of the dead. Now, there is a want of the other member which related to the pious, who acknowledged and received this benefit; but it is complete in regard to unbelievers, who received this announcement to their confusion. For when they saw but one redemption, from which they were excluded, what could they do but despair? I hear our opponents muttering, and saying that this is a gloss of my own invention, and that such authority does not bind them. I have no wish to bind them to my authority, I only ask them whether or not the spirits shut up in prison are spirits? There is another clearer passage in the same writer, when he says (1 Peter 4:6) that the gospel was preached to the dead, in order that they may be judged according to men in the flesh, but live according to God in the spirit. You see how, while the flesh is delivered over to death, life is claimed for the spirit. A relation is expressed between life and death, and, by antithesis, the one dies and the other lives.

We learn the same thing from Solomon, when describing man's death, he makes a wide difference between the soul and the body. He says,

"Until the dust return to the earth whence it was, and the spirit return to God who gave it." (Ecclesiastes 12:7)

I am aware that they are little affected by this argument, because they say that life returns to God, who is the fountain of life; and this is all. But the words themselves proclaim that in this way violence is done to them, and it is therefore needless to refute a silly quibble, which is unworthy of being either heard or read. Even this must imply, according to them, that souls return to the fountain of life only by a dream! Corresponding to this is a passage in Esdras, a writer whom I would not oppose to them did they not greatly lean upon him. Let them then hear their own Esdras, (4 Esdras 3:2) "The earth will render up those things which sleep in it, and dwell in silence; and the storehouses will render up the souls which committed to them." They triflingly allege that the "storehouses" are *Divine Providence,* and that "souls" are *thoughts,* so that the Book of Life is to exhibit thoughts in the presence of God. They evidently speak thus, merely because they are ashamed to be silent, and have nothing better to say. But if we may turn about the Scriptures in this way, everything may be perverted! Here, however, though I have ample supplies, I will not produce anything of my own, since the writer defends himself from this misinterpretation. A little before he had said, (Esdras 4:3,) "Did not the souls of these petition in their abodes, saying, How long do we hope this, O Lord? When will the harvest of our reward come?" What are these souls which petition and hope? Here, if they would escape, they must dig another burrow for themselves!

Let us come now to the history of the rich man and Lazarus, the latter of whom, after all the labors and toils of his mortal life are past, is at length carried into Abraham's bosom, while the former, having had his comforts here, now suffers torments. A great gulf is interposed between the joys of the one and the sufferings of the other. Are these mere dreams — the gates of ivory which the poets fable? To secure a means of escape, they make the history a parable, and say, that all which truth speaks concerning Abraham, the rich man and the poor man, is fiction. Such reverence do they pay to God and his word! Let them produce even one passage from Scripture where any one is called by name in a parable! What is meant by the words — "There was a poor man named Lazarus?" Either the Word of God must lie, or it is a true narrative.

This is observed by the ancient expounders of Scripture. Ambrose says — It is a narrative rather than a parable, inasmuch as the name is added. Gregory takes the same view. Certainly Tertullian, Irenaeus, Origen, Cyprian and Jerome, speak of it as a history. Among these, Tertullian thinks that, in the person of the rich man, Herod is designated, and in Lazarus John Baptist. The words of Irenaeus are "The Lord did not tell us a fable in the case of the rich man and Lazarus," etc, And Cyril, in replying to the Arians, who drew from it an argument against the Divinity of Christ, does not relate it as a parable, but expounds it as a history. (Tertull. lib. adv. Marcion; Iren. lib. 4: contra haeres, cap.

4; Origen, Hom. 5 in Ezech.; Cyprian epist, 3; Hieron. in Jes. c. 49 and 65; Hilar. in Psalm 3.; Cyril in John 1 chapter 22.) They are more absurd when they bring forward the name of Augustine, pretending that he held their view. They affirm this, I presume, because in one place he says — "In the parable, by Lazarus is to be understood Christ, and by the rich man the Pharisees;" when all he means is, that the narrative is converted into a parable if the person of Lazarus is assigned to Christ, and that of the rich man to the Pharisees. (August. de Genes. ad Liter. lib. 8:) This is the usual custom with those who take up a violent prejudice in favor of an opinion. Seeing that they have no ground to stand upon, they lay hold not only of syllables but letters to twist them to their use! To prevent them from insisting here, the writer himself elsewhere declares, that he understands it to be a history. Let them now go and try to put out the light of day by means of their smoke!

They cannot escape without always falling into the same net: for though we should grant it to be a parable, (this they cannot at all prove,) what more can they make of it than just that there is a comparison which must be founded in truth? If these great theologians do not know this, let them learn it from their grammars, there they will find that a parable is a similitude, founded on reality. Thus, when it is said that a certain man had two sons to whom he divided his goods, there must be in the nature of things both a man and sons, inheritance and goods. In short, the invariable rule in parables is, that we first conceive a simple subject and set it forth; then, from that conception, we are guided to the scope of the parable — in other words, to the thing itself to which it is accommodated. Let them imitate Chrysostom, who is their Achilles in this matter. He thought that it was a parable, though he often extracts a reality from it, as when he proves from it that the dead have certain abodes, and shews the dreadful nature of Gehenna, and the destructive effects of luxury. (Chrysos. Hom, 25 in Matthew Hom. 57; *in eundem,* In Par ad The. Lapsor. Hom. 4 Matthew) Not to lose many words here, let them consult common sense, if they have any, and they will easily perceive the nature and force of the parable.

Feeling desirous, as far as we can, to satisfy all, we will here say something respecting THE REST OF THE SOUL WHEN, IN SURE TRUST IN THE DIVINE PROMISE, IT IS FREED FROM THE BODY. Scripture, by the bosom of Abraham, only means to designate this rest. *First,* we give the name of "rest" to that which our opponents call "sleep." We have no aversion, indeed, to the term *sleep,* were it not corrupted and almost polluted by their falsehoods. *Secondly,* by "rest" we understand, not sloth, or lethargy, or anything like the drowsiness of ebriety which they attribute to the soul; but tranquillity of conscience and security, which always accompanies faith, but is never complete in all its parts till after death.

The Church, indeed, while still dwelling on the earth as a stranger, learns the blessedness of believers from the lips of the Lord, (Isaiah 32:18,) "My people will walk in the beauty of peace, and in the tents of trust, and in rich rest." She herself, on the other hand, giving thanks, sings to the Lord while blessing her, (Isaiah 26:12,)

"O Lord, thou wilt give us peace: for thou hast performed all our works for us."

Believers have this PEACE on receiving the gospel, when they see that God, whom they dreaded as their Judge, has become their Father; themselves, instead of children of wrath, children of grace; and the bowels of the divine mercy poured out toward them, so that now they expect from God nothing but goodness and mildness. But since human life on earth is a warfare, (Job 7:1,) those who feel both the stings of sin and the remains of the flesh, must feel depression in the world, though with consolation in God — such consolation, however, as does not leave the mind perfectly calm and undisturbed. But when they shall be divested of flesh and the desires of the flesh, (which, like domestic enemies, break their peace,) then at length will they rest and recline with God: For thus speaks the Prophet,

"The just perisheth, and no man layeth it to heart; and men of mercy are gathered: for the just is gathered from the face of wickedness. Let peace come, let him who hath walked under his direction rest in his bed." (Isaiah 57:1.)

Does he not call those to peace who had been the sons of peace? Still, as their peace was with God, and they had war in the world, he calls them to a higher degree of peace.

Accordingly, Ezekiel and John, when they would describe the throne of God's glory, encircle it with a rainbow, which we know to be the sign of the covenant between God and men. This John has taught more clearly in another passage,

"Blessed are the dead who die in the Lord, yea, says the Scripture, that they may rest from their labors." (Ezekiel 1:28; Revelation 9:3; 14:13.)

This, then, is the bosom of Abraham: for it was he himself who, with ready mind, embraced the promises made to his own seed, never doubting that the word of God was efficacious and true: and as if God had actually performed what he had promised, he waited for that blessed seed with no less assurance than if he had had it in his hands, and perceived it with all his senses. Accordingly, our Lord bore this testimony to him, that "he saw His day and was glad." (John 8:56.) Here is the peace of Abraham, here his rest, here his sleep; only let not an honorable name be polluted by the lips of these dull sleepers: for in what can *conscience* rest more pleasantly than in this peace, which opens to it the treasures of heavenly grace and intoxicates it with the sweetness of the Lord's cup? Why, O sleepers! when you hear of intoxication, do you not think of vertigo, of heaviness, of your gross carnal sleep? Such are the inconveniences which ensue upon intoxication! Such may be your gross imaginations; but those who are taught of God understand that "sleep" is used, in this way, for the peace of conscience which the Lord bestows upon his followers in the abode of peace, and "intoxication" for the riches with which God satisfies his people in the abode of opulence. If Abraham possessed this peace when exposed to inroads from his enemies, to labors and dangers, nay, when bearing about with him his flesh, a domestic enemy than whom there is none more pernicious, how great must his peace be now that he has escaped from all hostile blows and darts?

No one can now wonder why the elect of God are said to "rest in the bosom of Abraham," when they have passed from this life to their God! It is just because they are admitted with Abraham, the father of the faithful, where they enjoy God fully without weariness. Wherefore, not without reason, Augustine says in a certain place, "As we call eternal life, so we may also call PEACE 'The end of the blessed:' for He can give nothing better who can give nothing greater or better than himself, being THE GOD OF PEACE. (August. de Civit. lib. 19.)

Henceforth, when the "bosom of Abraham" is spoken of, let them not wrest it to their dream, since the truth of Scripture at once establishes and condemns their vanity. There is, I say, a rest, a heavenly Jerusalem, *i.e.,* a vision of peace, in which the God of peace gives himself to be seen by his peace-makers, according to the promise of Christ. How often does the Spirit make mention of this *peace* in Scripture, and use the figure of "sleeping" and "resting" so familiarly, that the use of no figure is more frequent! "Thy saints," says David, "will exult, they will rejoice in their beds." (Psalm 149:5; Isaiah 57:2.) Another says,

"Thy dead shall live, thy slain shall rise again. Awake, and praise, ye dwellers in the dust, because thy dew is the dew of meadows, and thou shalt bring the land of giants to destruction." "Go, my people, enter into thy tabernacles, shut thy doors upon thee, hide thyself for a little, until the indignation be overpast." (1 Corinthians 15:12; 1 Thessalonians 5:13; Matthew 5:8, 9; Isaiah 26:19.) Nay, the Hebrew tongue uses the word to signify any security and confidence. David, on the other hand, says,

"I will sleep, and rest in peace." (Psalm 4:9.)

And the Prophet says,

"I will make a covenant, in that day, with the beast of the field, and with the bird of the air, and with the reptile of the earth; I will break the bow and the sword, and banish war from the earth, and make them to sleep without terror." (Hosea 2:18.)

And Moses says,

"I will give peace in your borders, and not one shall be afraid." (Leviticus 26:6.)

And in the book of Job it is said,

"Thou shalt have confidence in the hope set before thee, and buried wilt sleep secure. Thou shalt rest, and there will be none to terrify thee, and very many will supplicate thy face." (Job 11:18, 19.)

Of the same thing we are admonished by the Latin proverb, of "sleeping on both ears," meaning to live securely. The souls of the living, therefore, who rest in the word of the Lord, and desire not to anticipate the will of their God, but are ready to follow wherever he may invite, keep themselves under his hand, sleep, and have peace. The command given to them is,

"If His truth tarry, wait for it." (Habakkuk 2:3.)

And again,

"In hope and silence will be your strength." (Isaiah 30:15.)

Now, when they wait for something which they see not, and desire what they have not, it is evident that their peace is imperfect. On the other hand, while they confidently expect what they do expect, and in faith desire what they desire, it is clear that their desire is tranquil. This peace is increased and advanced by death, which, freeing, and as it were discharging them from the warfare of this world, leads them into the place of peace, where, while wholly intent on beholding God, they have nothing better to which they can turn their eyes or direct their desire. Still, something is wanting which they desire to see, namely, the complete and perfect glory of God, to which they always aspire. Though there is no impatience in their desire, their rest is not yet full and perfect, since he is said to rest who is where he desires to be; and the measure of desire has no end till it has arrived where it was tending. But if the eyes of the elect look to the supreme glory of God as their final good, their desire is always moving onward till the glory of God is complete, and this completion awaits the judgment day. Then will be verified the saying,

"I will be satisfied, when I awake, with beholding thy countenance." (Psalm 17:15.)

Not to omit the reprobate, whose doom need not give us great concern, I would like our opponents candidly to tell me, On what ground they have any hope of RESURRECTION, unless it be because Christ rose? He is the first-begotten of the dead, and the first-fruits of them that rise again. As he died and rose again, so do we also die and rise again. For if the death to which we were liable was to be overcome by death, he undoubtedly suffered the same death as we do, and likewise in death suffered what we suffer. Scripture makes this plain when it calls him the first-begotten of the dead, and the first-fruits of them that rise again. (Colossians 1:18.) And it thus teaches, that believers in the midst of death acknowledge him as their leader, and while they behold their death sanctified by his death, have no dread of its curse. This Paul intimates when he says, that he was made conformable to his death, until he should attain to the resurrection of the dead. (Philippians 2:20.) This conformity, here begun by the cross, He followed out until He should complete it by death.

Now, O dreamy sleepers, commune with your own hearts, and consider how Christ died. Did He sleep when he was working for your salvation? Not thus does he say of himself,

"As the Father hath life in himself, so hath he given to the Son to have life in himself." (John 5:26.)

How could he who has life in himself lose it?

Let them not tell me that these things belong to his Divinity. For if there has been given to him who has not, it has been given to man and not to God to have life in himself. For seeing that Jesus Christ is Son of God and man, that which he is by nature as God is he also by grace as man, that thus we may all receive of his fullness, and grace for grace. When men hear that there is life with God, what hope can they conceive from it, while they at the same time know that by their sins; a cloud is interposed between them and God? But it is surely great consolation to know that God the Father has anointed Christ with the oil of joy above his fellows — that the man Christ has received from the Father gifts for men, so that we may be able to find life in our nature. Hence we read that the multitude, after the boy was raised, glorified God who had given such power to men. (Acts 20:12.) This was certainly seen by Cyril, who agrees with us in the exposition of this passage. But when we say that Christ, as man, has life in himself, we do not say that he is the cause of life to himself.

This may be made plain from a familiar comparison. A fountain from which all drink, and from which streams flow and are derived, is said to have water in itself; and yet it has it not of itself but of the source, which constantly supplies what may suffice both for the running streams and the men who drink of it. Accordingly, Christ has life in himself, i.e., fullness of life, by which he both himself lives and quickens others; yet he has it not of himself, as he elsewhere declares that he lives by the Father. And though as God he had life in himself, yet when he assumed human nature, he received from the Father the gift of having life in himself in that nature also. These things give us the fullest assurance that Christ could not be extinguished by death, even in respect of his human nature; and that although he was truly and naturally delivered to the death which we all undergo, he, however, always retained the gift of the Father. True! death was a separation of soul and body. But the soul never lost its life. Having been commended to the Father it could not but be safe.

This is intimated by the words in Peter's sermon, in which he affirms that it was impossible he could be holden of death, in order that the Scripture might be fulfilled,

"Thou wilt not leave my soul in hell, nor allow thy Holy One to see corruption." (Acts 2:27.)

Though we should grant that in this prophecy "soul" is used for life, Christ asks and expects two things of his Father — not to abandon his soul to perdition, nor allow himself to be subjected to corruption. This was fulfilled. For his soul was supported by divine power, and did not fall into perdition, and the body was preserved in the tomb till its Resurrection. All

these things Peter embraced in one expression, when he says
that Christ could not be held of death kratei~sqai, *i.e.,* yield to
the domination, or fall under the power of death, or continue to
be seized by it. It is true that Peter, in that discourse, leaving off
the consideration of the soul, continues to speak of the
incorruption of the body only. This he does to convince the
Jews, on the authority of their own writers, that this prophecy
did not apply to David, whose sepulcher was extant among
them, whose body they knew to have fallen under corruption, so
that they could not deny the resurrection of our Lord. Another
proof of the immortality of his soul was given us by our Savior,
when he made the confinement of Jonah three days within the
whale's belly to be a type of his death, stating that thus he would
be three days and three nights in the belly of the earth. But
Jonah cried unto the Lord from the belly of the fish, and was
heard. That belly is death. He therefore had his soul safe in
death, and by means of it could cry unto the Lord.

Isaac, also, who was a type of Christ, and was restored to his
father from death, by a kind of type of the resurrection, as the
Apostle says, shews us the truth in a figure. For after having
been bound, and placed upon the altar as a prepared victim, he
was loosed by the order of God. But the ram which had been
caught in the thicket was substituted for Isaac. And why is it that
Isaac does not die, but just because Christ has given immortality
to that which is peculiar to man — I mean the soul? But the
ram, the irrational animal which is given up to death in his stead,
is the body. In the binding of Isaac is represented the soul,
which showed only a semblance, of dying in the death of Christ,
and the same is daily exhibited in ordinary instances of death.
But as the soul of Christ was set free from prison, so our souls
also are set free before they perish. Let any one of you now put
on a supercilious air, and pretend that the death of Christ was a
sleep — or let him go over and join the camp of Apollinaris!
Christ was indeed awake when he exerted himself for your

salvation; but you sleep your sleep, and, buried in the darkness of blindness, give no heed to his wakening calls!

Besides, it not only consoles us to think that Christ, our Head, did not perish in the shadow of death, but we have the additional security of his Resurrection, by which he constituted himself the Lord of death, and raised all of us who have any part in him above death, so that Paul did not hesitate to say, that "our life is hid with Christ in God." (Colossians 3:3.) Elsewhere he says, "I live, yet not I, but; Christ liveth in me." (Galatians 2:20.) What remains for our opponents but to cry with open mouth that Christ sleeps in sleeping souls? For if Christ lives in them he also dies in them. If, therefore, the life of Christ is ours, let him who insists that our life is ended by death, pull Christ down from the right hand of the Father and consign him to the second death. If He can die, our death is certain; if he has no end of life, neither can our souls ingrafted in him be ended by any death!

But why labor the point? Is there any obscurity in the words,

"Because I live, ye shall live also?" (John 14:19.)

If we live because he lives, then if we die he does not live. Is there any obscurity in his promise, that he will remain in all who are united to him by faith, and they in him? (John 6:56.) Therefore, if we would deprive the members of life, let us dissever them from Christ. Our confession, which is sufficiently established, is this,

"In Adam all die, but in Christ are made alive." (1 Corinthians 15:22.)

These things are splendidly and magnificently handled by Paul. (Romans 8:10.) "If the Spirit of Christ dwell in us, the body is dead because of sin, but the Spirit is life because of righteousness." He no doubt calls the body the mass of sin, which resides in man from the native property of the flesh; and the spirit the part of man spiritually regenerated. Wherefore, when a little before he deplored his wretchedness because of the remains of sin adhering to him, (Romans 7:24) he did not desire to be taken away altogether, or to be nothing, in order that he might escape from that misery, but to be freed from the body of death, i.e., that the mass of sin in him might die, that the spirit, being purged, and, as it were, freed from dregs, he might have peace with God through this very circumstance; declaring, that his better part was held captive by bodily chains and would be freed by death.

I wish we could with true faith perceive of what nature the kingdom of God is which exists in believers, even while they are in this life. For it would at the same time be easy to understand that eternal life is begun. He who cannot deceive promised thus:
—

" Whoso hears my words has eternal life, and does not come into condemnation, but hath passed from death unto life." (John 5:24.)

If an entrance has been given into eternal life, why do they interrupt it by death? Elsewhere he says,

"This is the work of the Father, that every one who believes in the Son may not perish, but have eternal life; and I will raise him up at the last day." (John 6:40.)

Again,

"He who eats my flesh, and drinks my blood, hath eternal life; and I will raise him up at the last day. Not as your fathers did eat manna in the wilderness and are dead. He who eateth of this bread shall live for ever." (John 6:54.)

Do not attempt here to introduce your fictitious comments concerning The Last Day. He promises us two things — Eternal life, and the Resurrection. Though you are told of two you admit only one! Another expression of Christ is still more decisive. He says,

"I am the resurrection and the life. He who believeth on me shall live though he were dead. And whoso liveth and believeth in me shall not die for ever." (John 11:25, 26.)

It will not do to say, that those who are raised do not die for ever. Our Lord meant not only this, but that it is impossible they can ever die. This meaning is better expressed by the Greek words eijv to<n aijw~na equivalent in Latin to *in seculum:* for when we say that a thing will not be *in seculum,* we affirm that it will never be at all. Thus in another passage, "Whoso will keep my word shall not see death for ever." (John 8:51.) This invincibly proves, that he who will keep the word of the Lord shall not see death; and it should be sufficient to arm the faith of Christians against the perverseness of these men. This is our belief, this our expectation. Meanwhile, what remains for them but to continue sleeping on till they are awakened by the clang of the trumpet which shall break their slumbers like a thief in the night?

And if God is the life of the soul, just as the soul is the life of the body, how can it be that the soul keeps acting upon the body so long as it is in the body, and never is for an instant idle, and yet that God should cease from acting as if He, were fatigued! If such is the vigor of the soul in sustaining, moving, and impelling a lump of clay, how great must be the energy of God in moving and actuating the soul to which agility is natural! Some go the length of saying, that the soul becomes evanescent; others, that its vigor is not exercised after the fetters of the body are dissolved. What answer then will they give to David's hymn,

(Psalm 73,) wherein he describes the beginning, middle, and end of the life of the blessed? He says, "They will go from strength to strength; the Lord of hosts will be seen in Zion;" or, as the Hebrew has it, from abundance to abundance,. If they always increase till they see God, and pass from that increase to the vision of God, on what ground do these men bury them in drunken slumber and deep sloth?

The same thing is testified still more clearly by the Apostle when he says, that if they are dissolved they are no longer able to resist the Spirit of God. His words are,

"We know that if the earthly house of this tabernacle were dissolved, we have a building of God, a house not made with hands, eternal in the heavens. For in this we groan, desiring to be clothed upon with our house which is from heaven; if so be that being clothed we shall not be found naked. For we who are in this tabernacle do groan being burdened, not because we wish to be unclothed, but clothed upon, that mortality may be swallowed up of life." (2 Corinthians 5:1-3.)

A little afterwards he says,

"Therefore we are always of good courage, and know that while we are at home in the body we are absent from the Lord; (for we walk by faith, not by sight;) we are confident, and would rather be absent from the body and present with the Lord." (2 Corinthians 5:6-8)

Here the evasion they have recourse to is, that the Apostle's words refer to The Day of Judgment, when both we shall be clothed upon, and mortality shall be swallowed up of life. Accordingly, they say, the Apostle includes both in one paragraph,

"We must all appear before the judgment-seat of Christ." (2 Corinthians 5:10.)

But why do they refer this clothing upon to the body, rather than to spiritual blessings with which we are richly supplied at death? What forces them to interpret the life there spoken of as meaning *resurrection?* The simple and obvious meaning of the Apostle is, We desire indeed to depart from this prison of the body, but not to wander uncertain without a home: There is a better home which the Lord hath prepared for us; clothed with it, we shall not be found naked. Christ is our clothing, and our armor is that which the Apostle puts upon us. (Ephesians 6:11.) And it is written, (Psalm 45:13,) "The king will admire the beauty of his spouse, who will be richly provided with gifts, and all glorious within." In fine, the Lord has put a seal upon his own people, whom he will acknowledge both at death and at the resurrection. (Revelation 7) Why do they not rather look back to what he had just said in the previous context., with which he connects this very sentence?

"Though our outward man decays, our inward man is renewed day by day." (2 Corinthians 4:16.)

They find it more difficult to evade what the Apostle subjoins as to our appearance before the judgment-seat of Christ, after having said, that whether at home or living abroad we labor to please him. Since by *home* he means the body, what are we to understand by this *living abroad?*

Therefore, though we were not to add one word, the meaning is obvious without an interpreter. It is, that both in the body and out of the body we labor to please the Lord; and that we shall perceive the presence of God when we shall be separated from this body — that we will no longer walk by faith but by sight, since the load of clay by which we are pressed down, acts as a

kind of wall of partition, keeping us far away from God. Those
triflers, on the contrary, absurdly pretend that at death we are to
be more widely separated from God than we are during life! In
regard even to the present life, it is said of the righteous, "They
shall walk, O Lord, in the light of thy countenance," (Psalm 88;)
and again,

"The Spirit himself beareth witness with our spirit that we are
the children of God," (Romans 8:16 ;)

besides many other passages to the same effect. But these men
deprive the righteous at death both of the light of God's
countenance and the witness of his Spirit; and, therefore, if they
are correct, we are happier now than we are to be at death! For,
as Paul says, (Philippians 3,) even while we live under the
elements of this world, we have a habitation and citizenship in
the heavens. But if, as they maintain, our souls are at death
overwhelmed with lethargy, and buried in oblivion, they must
lose every kind of spiritual enjoyment which they previously
possessed.

We are better taught by the Sacred Writings. The body, which
decays, weighs down the soul, and confining it within an earthly
habitation, greatly limits its perceptions. If the body is the prison
of the soul, if the earthly habitation is a kind of fetters, what is
the state of the soul when set free from this prison, when loosed
from these fetters? Is it not restored to itself, and as it were
made complete, so that we may truly say, that all which it gains is
so much lost to the body? Whether they will or not, they must
be forced to confess, that when we put off the load of the body,
the war between the spirit and the flesh ceases. In short, the
mortification of the flesh is the quickening of the spirit. Then
the soul, set free from impurities, is truly spiritual, so as to be in
accordance with the will of God, and not subject to the tyranny
of the flesh, rebelling against it. In short, the mortification of the
flesh will be the quickening of the spirit: For then the soul,

having shaken off all kinds of pollution, is truly spiritual, so that it consents to the will of God, and is no longer subjected to the tyranny of the flesh; thus dwelling in tranquillity, with all its thoughts fixed on God. Are we to say that it sleeps, when it can rise aloft unencumbered with any load? — that it slumbers, when it can perceive many things by sense and thought, no obstacle preventing? These things not only manifest the errors of these men, but also their malignant hostility to the works and operations which the Scriptures proclaim that God performs in his saints.

We acknowledge God as growing in his elect, and increasing from day to day. This the wise man teaches us, when he says, (Proverbs 4:18,) "The path of the just is as the light, increasing into the perfect day." And the Apostle affirms, that

"He who has begun a good work in you will perfect it against the day of the Lord Jesus." (Philippians 1:6.)

These men not only intermit the work of God for a time, but even extinguish it. Those who formerly went from faith to faith, from virtue to virtue, and enjoyed a foretaste of blessedness when they exercised themselves in thinking of God, they deprive both of faith and virtue, and all thought of God, and merely place on beds, in a sluggish and lethargic state! For how do they interpret that progress? Do they think that souls are perfected when they are made heavy with sleep as a preparation for their being brought sleek and fat into the presence of God when he shall sit in judgment? Had they a particle of sense they would not prattle thus absurdly about the soul, but would make all the difference between a celestial soul and an earthly body, that there is between heaven and earth. When the Apostle longs to depart and to be with Christ, (Philippians 1:23,) do they think he wishes to fall asleep so as no longer to feel any desire of Christ? Was this all he was longing for when he said he knew he had a building of God, an house not made with hands, as soon as the earthly house of his tabernacle should be dissolved? (2 Corinthians 5:1.) Where were the benefit of being with Christ were he to cease to live the life of Christ?

What! are they not overawed by the words of the Lord when, calling himself the God of Abraham, Isaac, and Jacob, he says, he is

"God not of the dead but of the living?" (Matthew 22:32.)

Is He, then, neither to be to them a God, nor are they to be to him a people? (Mark 12:27.) But they say that these things will be realized when the dead shall be raised to life. Although the question expressly asked is, Have you not read what was said concerning the Resurrection of the dead? this evasion will not serve their purpose. Christ having to do with the Sadducees, who denied not only the Resurrection of the dead but the immortality of the soul, convicts them of two errors by this single expression. For if God is God not of the dead but of the living, and Abraham, Isaac, and Jacob had departed this life when God spoke to Moses calling himself their God, the inference is, that they were living another life. Those must surely be in being of whom God says that he is their God. Hence Luke adds, "For all things live to him, (Luke 30:28,) not meaning that all things live by the presence of God, but by his energy. It follows, therefore, that Abraham, Isaac, and Jacob are alive. To this passage we add that of the Apostle, (Romans 14:8, 9,) "Whether we live, we live unto the Lord, whether we die, we die unto the Lord: whether we live or die, we are the Lord's. For, for this Christ both died and rose again, that he might be Lord of the living and the dead." What more solid foundation could there be on which to rear our faith, than to say that Christ rules over the dead? There can only be rule over persons who exist, the exercise of government necessarily implying the existence of subjects.

Testimony is also borne against them in heaven before God and his angels, by the souls of the martyrs under the altar, who with loud voice cry,

"How long, O Lord, dost thou not avenge our blood on those who dwell on the earth? And there were given unto them white robes, and it was told them still to rest for a season, until the number of their fellow-servants and their brethren who were to be slain like them should be completed." (Revelation 6:10, 11.)

The souls of the dead cry aloud, and white robes are given unto them! O sleeping spirits! what are white robes to you? Are they pillows on which you are to lie down and sleep? You see that white robes are not at all adapted for sleep, and therefore, when thus clothed, they must be awake. If this is true, these white robes undoubtedly designate the commencement of glory, which the Divine liberality bestows upon martyrs while waiting for the day of judgment.

It is no new thing for Scripture to designate glory, festivity, and joy, under the figure of a white robe. It was in a white robe the Lord appeared in vision to Daniel. In this garb the Lord was seen on Mount Tabor. The angel of the Lord appeared to the women at the sepulcher in white raiment; and under the same form did the angels appear to the disciples as they continued gazing up to heaven after their Lord's ascension. In the same, too, did the angel appear to Cornelius, and when the son who had wasted his substance had returned to his father, he was clothed in the best robe, as a symbol of joy and festivity. (Daniel 7:9; Matthew 17:2; 28:3; Mark 16:5; Acts 1:10; 10:30; Luke 15:22.)

Again, If the souls of the dead cried aloud, they were not sleeping. When, then; did that drowsiness overtake them? Let no one here obtrude the expression that "the blood of Abel cried

for vengeance!" I am perfectly ready to admit that when blood
has been shed, it is an ordinary figure to represent it as calling
aloud for vengeance. In this passage, however, it is certain that
the feeling of the martyrs is represented to us by crying, because
their desire is expressed and their petition described without any
figure, "How long, O Lord, dost thou not avenge?" etc.
Accordingly, in the same book John has described a twofold
Resurrection as well as a twofold death; namely, one of the soul
before judgment, and another when the body will be raised up,
and when the soul also will be raised up to glory. "Blessed," says
he, "are those who have part in the first Resurrection; on them
the second death takes no effect." (Revelation 20:6.) Well, then,
may you be afraid who refuse to acknowledge that first
Resurrection, which, however, is the only entrance to beatific
glory.

One of the most fatal blows to the dogma of these men is the
answer which was given to the thief who implored mercy. He
prayed, "Lord, remember me when thou comest to thy
kingdom;" and he hears the reply, "Today shalt thou be with me
in paradise." (Luke 22:42.) He who is everywhere, promises that
he will be present with the thief. And he promises paradise,
because he who thus enjoys God has fulness of delight. Nor
does he put him off for a long series of days. He calls him to the
joys of his kingdom on that very day! They endeavor to evade
the force of our Savior's expression by a paltry quibble. They
say, "One day is with him as a thousand years." (2 Peter 3:8.) But
they remember not that God in speaking to man, accommodates
himself to human sense. They are not told that in Scripture one
day is used for a thousand years. Who would listen to the
expounder, who, on being told that God would do something
today, should immediately explain it as meaning thousands of
years? When Jonah declared to the Ninevites,

"Forty days and Nineveh shall be destroyed," (Jonah 3:4,)

might they have waited securely for the future judgment, as not to be inflicted till forty thousand years should have elapsed? It was not in this sense Peter said, that in the sight of God a thousand years were as one day; but when some false prophets counted days and hours for the purpose of charging God with falsehood in not fulfilling His promises, the moment they wished for it, he reminds them that with God is eternity, compared with which a thousand years are scarcely a single moment.

Feeling themselves completely entangled, they maintain that in Scripture *Today* means the duration of the New, and *Yesterday* the duration of the Old Testament! To this meaning they wrest the passage, (Hebrews 13:8,) "Jesus Christ, yesterday, and today, the same for ever." Here they are totally in error. For, if he was only *Yesterday*, then not being before the commencement of the Old Testament, he might at one time have begun to be! Where then will be Jesus, the eternal God, in respect of humanity, even the first-born of every creature, and the Lamb slain from the foundation of the world? (Colossians 1:15; Revelation 13:8.) Again, if *Today* means the time which intervenes between the incarnation of Christ and the day of judgment, we hold that paradise will be enjoyed by the thief previous to the period at which they say that souls are awakened out of sleep! Thus, then, they will be forced to confess that the promise given to the thief was fulfilled before the judgment, though they at the same time insist that it was not to be fulfilled till after the judgment. But if they confine the expression to the time which follows the judgment, why does the author of the Epistle add *"For ever?"* And to make their darkness visible, if Christ referred in that promise to the period of judgment, he ought not to have said, *Today*, but at a future age; just as Isaiah, when he wished to express the mystery of the Resurrection, called Christ "the Father of the future age." (Isaiah 9:6.)

But since the Apostle used the expression, "Yesterday, today, and for ever," for what we are accustomed to express by "Was, is, and shall be" — the three tenses being with us equivalent to eternity — what more do they by their quibble than pervert the Apostle's meaning? That the term *Yesterday* is used to comprehend an eternal duration may be distinctly learned from the Prophet, who writes, (Isaiah 30:33) "Tophet has been ordained for the wicked from the time of yesterday," while we know from the words of Christ that fire has been prepared from eternity for the devil and his angels. (Matthew 25:41.) All of them who have any judgment or sound mind, here see that they have no means left by which they can elude the truth made thus manifest. Still, however, they continue to cavil and say, that paradise was promised to the thief on that day, just as death was denounced to our first parents on the day on which they should taste of the tree of the knowledge of good and evil. Were we to grant this, we can still force them to admit that the robber on that day was restored from the misery into which Adam fell on the day on which he transgressed the law that had been laid upon him. Moreover, when I shall by and bye discourse of death, I shall make it abundantly plain, if I mistake not, how our parents did die on the day on which they rebelled against God.

Let me now direct my discourse to those who with a pure conscience, remembering the promises of God, acquiesce in them. Brethren, let no man rob you of this faith, though all the gates of hell should resist, since you have the assurance of God, who cannot deny his truth! There is not the least obscurity in his language to the Church, while still a pilgrim on the earth:

"You shall no more have the sun to shine by day, nor shall the moon illumine you by her brightness, for the Lord shall be your everlasting light." (Isaiah 60:19.)

Here if they, after their usual custom, refer us to the last resurrection, it will be easy to refute the absurdity from individual expressions of the chapter, in which the Lord at one time promises his Messiah, and at another promises to admit the Gentiles to alliance, etc. Let us ever call to mind what the Spirit hath taught by the mouth of David, (Psalm 92:13) "The just shall flourish like the palm-tree, he shall be multiplied like the cedar on Lebanon. Those who have been planted in the house of the Lord will flourish in the courts of our God, they will still bud forth in their old age, they will be fat and flourishing."

Be not alarmed because all the powers of nature are thought to fail at the very time when you hear of a budding and flourishing old age. Reflecting with yourselves on these things, let your souls, in unison with David's, exclaim, (Psalm 103:5,) "O my soul, bless the Lord, who satisfieth thy mouth with good: thy youth shall be renewed like the eagle's." Leave the rest to the Lord, who guards our entrance and our exit from this time forth even for evermore. He it is who sendeth the early and the latter rain upon his elect. Of him we have been told, "Our God is the God of salvation," and "to the Lord our God belong the issues of death." Christ expounded this goodness of the Father to us when he said, "Father, with regard to those whom thou hast given me, I will that where I am they also may be with me, that they may behold my glory which thou hast given me." (Psalm 121:8; Joel 2:23; Psalm 68:20; John 17:24.)

The faith thus sustained by all prophecies, evangelical truth, and Christ himself, let us hold fast — the faith that our spirit is the image of God, like whom it lives, understands, and is eternal. As long as it is in the body it exerts its own powers; but when it quits this prison-house it returns to God, whose presence, it meanwhile enjoys while it rests in the hope of a blessed Resurrection. This rest is its paradise. On the other hand, the spirit of the reprobate, while it waits for the dreadful judgment, is tortured by that anticipation, which the Apostle for that reason calls fobera>n, (fearful.) To inquire beyond this is to

plunge into the abyss of the Divine mysteries. It is enough to
have learned what the Spirit, our best Teacher, deemed it
sufficient to have taught. His words are,

"Hear me, and your soul shall live." (Isaiah 4:8.)

How wisely, in opposition to the vanity and arrogance of
those men, was it said, "The souls of the righteous are in the
hands of God, and the pangs of death will not touch them. To
the eyes of the foolish they seemed to die, but they are in peace,"
etc. This is the end of our wisdom, which, while it is sober and
subject to God, at the same time knows, that those who aspire
higher only procure a fall.

Let us now examine the cradle in which they rock souls asleep,
and let us dispose of the soporiferous draught which they give
them to drink. They carry about with them some passages of
Scripture which seem to favor that SLEEP, and then, as if the
fact of *sleeping* were clearly proved, fulminate against those who
do not instantly subscribe to their error. They insist, *first,* That
God did not infuse into man any other soul than that which is
common to him with the brutes; for Scripture ascribes the same
"living soul" to all alike; as where it is said,

"God created the great whales and every living soul." (Genesis
2:21.)

Again,

"To each of all flesh in which was the breath of life," (Genesis
7:15)

and other things to the same effect. And it is said, that even had
the Sacred Writings elsewhere made no mention of the matter,
we are distinctly reminded by the Apostle, (1 Corinthians 15:42,)
that that living soul differs in no respect from the present life

with which the body vegetates, when he says, "It is sown in corruption, it will rise in incorruption; it is sown in weakness, it will rise in power; it is sown an animal, it will rise a spiritual body; as it is written, The first Adam was made a living soul, the last Adam a quickening spirit."

I admit that a *living soul* is repeatedly attributed to the brutes, because they, too, have their own life; but they live after one way, man after another. Man has a living soul by which he knows and understands; they have a living soul which gives their body sense and motion. Seeing, then, that the soul of man possesses reason, intellect, and will — qualities which are not annexed to the body — it is not wonderful that it subsists without the body, and does not perish like the brutes, which have nothing more than their bodily senses. Hence Paul was not ashamed to adopt the expression of a heathen poet, and call us the offspring of God. (Acts 17:28.) Let them, then, if they will, make a living soul common to man and to the brutes, since in so far as the body is concerned they have all the same life, but let them not employ this as an argument for confounding the soul of man with the brutes.

Nor let them obtrude upon me the Apostle's expression, which is more with me than against me. He says,

"The first Adam was a living soul, the last Adam a quickening spirit." (1 Corinthians 15:45.)

His answer here corresponds to the question of those who could not be persuaded of the Resurrection. They objected, How will the dead rise again? With what body will they come? The Apostle, to meet this objection, thus addresses them: If we learn by experience that the seed, which lives, grows, and yields fruit, has previously died, why may not the body after it has died rise again like a seed? And if dry and bare grain, after it has died, produces more abundant increase, by a wondrous virtue which God has implanted in it, why may not the body, by the same divine power, be raised better than it died? And that you may not wonder at this: How is it that man lives, but just because he was formed a living soul? This soul, however, though for a time it actuates and sustains the bodily mass, does not impart to it immortality or incorruption, and as long even as it exerts its own energy; it is not sufficient by itself, without the auxiliaries of food, drink, sleep, which are the signs of corruption; nor does it maintain it in a constant and uniform state without being subject to various kinds of inclinations. But when Christ shall have received us into his own glory, not only will the animal body be quickened by the soul, but made spiritual in a manner which our mind can neither comprehend nor our tongue express. (See Tertullian and August., Ep. 3, ad Fortunat.) You see, then, that in the Resurrection we shall be not a *different thing*, but a *different person*, (pardon the expression.) These things have been said of the body, to which the soul ministers life under the elements of this world; but when the fashion of this world shall have passed away, participation in the glory of God will exalt it above nature.

We now have the genuine meaning of the Apostle's expression. Augustine, having once erred in expounding it, as those men now do, afterwards acknowledged his error, and inserted it among his Retractations. In another place he treats the whole subject with the greatest distinctness. (Retract., c. 10, Ep. 146, Consentio.) I will make a few extracts : — "The soul indeed lives in an animal body, but does not quicken it so as to take away corruption; but when, in a spiritual body, adhering perfectly to the Lord, one spirit is formed, it so quickens it as to make it a spiritual body, consuming all corruption, fearing no separation." In short, were I to grant them all they ask in regard to a living soul, (on which expression, as I have already said, I do not found much,) yet that seat of the image of God always remains safe, whether they call it *"soul"* or *"spirit,"* or give it any other name.

It is not more difficult to refute their Objection taken from Ezekiel 37:9, where the Prophet, making a kind of supposititious Resurrection, calls a spirit from the four winds to breathe upon the dry bones. From this they think themselves entitled to infer, that the soul of man is nothing else than the power and faculty of motion without substance — a power and faculty which may become evanescent at death, and be again gathered together at the Resurrection. As if I might not in the same way infer that the Spirit of God is either wind or evanescent motion, seeing that Ezekiel himself, in his first vision, uses the term *"wind"* for the eternal Spirit of God! But to any man not altogether stupid it is easy to give the solution, though these good folks, from dulness or ignorance, observe it not. In both passages we see examples of what is ever and anon occurring in the Prophets, who figure spiritual things too high for human sense by corporeal and visible symbols. Accordingly, when Ezekiel wished to give a distinct and, as it were, bodily representation of the Spirit of God and the spirit of man — a thing altogether impossible in regard to a spiritual nature — he borrowed a similitude from corporeal objects to serve as a kind of image.

Their *second* Objection is, That the Soul, though endowed with immortality, lapsed into sin, and thereby sunk and destroyed its immortality. This was the appointed punishment for sin as denounced to our first parents — "Dying ye shall die." (Genesis 2:17.) And Paul says, "The wages of sin is death." (Romans 6:23.) And the Prophet exclaims, that "The soul that sinneth shall die." (Ezekiel 18:4.) They quote other similar passages. But I ask, *first,* Whether the same wages of sin were not paid to the Devil? — and yet his death was not such as to prevent him from being always awake, going about seeking whom he may devour, and working in the children of disobedience. I ask, *secondly,* Whether or not there is to be any end to that death? If none, as we must certainly acknowledge, then, although dead, they shall still feel eternal fire and the worm which dieth not. These things make it manifest that the immortality of the soul, which we assert, and which we say consists in a perception of good and evil, exists even when it is dead, and that that death is something else than the annihilation to which they would reduce it.

Nor are the Scriptures silent on this point, could they bring their mind to submit their own views to Scripture, instead of arrogantly affirming whatever their dark and drowsy brains may dictate. When God pronounces this sentence against man as a sinner, "Dust thou art, and to dust shalt thou return," does he say more than that that which has been taken from the earth shall return to the earth? Whither then does the soul go? Does it descend into the tomb, to rottenness and corruption? These points will be considered more fully by and bye. But now, why do they quibble? We have heard that that which is of the earth is to be returned to the earth. Why do we plunge the spirit of man under the earth? He says not that man will return to the earth, but that he who is dust will return to dust. But dust is that which was formed out of clay. It returns to dust, but not the spirit, which God derived from another quarter, and gave to man. Accordingly, we read in the book of Job,

"Remember how thou hast made me of clay, and will reduce me to dust." (Job 10:9.)

This is said of the body. A little after he adds,

"Life and mercy hast thou given me, and thy visitation has preserved my spirit." (Job 10:12.)

That life, then, was not to return to dust.

THE DEATH OF THE SOUL is very different. It is the judgment of God, the weight of which the wretched soul cannot bear without being wholly confounded, crushed, and desperate, as both the Scriptures teach us, and experience has taught those whom God has once smitten with his terrors. To begin with Adam, who first received the fatal wages, What do we think his feelings must have been when he heard the dreadful question, "Adam, where art thou?" It is easier to imagine than to express it, though imagination must fall far short of the reality. As the sublime majesty of God cannot be expressed in words, so neither can his dreadful anger on those on whom he inflicts it be expressed. They see the power of the Almighty actually present: to escape it, they would plunge themselves into a thousand abysses; but escape they cannot. Who does not confess that this is very death? Here I again say that they have no need of words who have at any time felt the stings of conscience; and let those who have not felt them only listen to the Scriptures, in which "our God" is described as "a consuming fire," and as slaying when he speaks in judgment. Such they knew him to be, who said, (Exodus 20:19; Deuteronomy 18:16,) "Let not the Lord speak to us, lest we die!"

Would you know what the death of the soul is? It is to be without God — to be abandoned by God, and left to itself: for if God is its life, it loses its life when it loses the presence of God. That which has been said in general may be shown in particular parts. If without God, there are no rays to illumine our night, surely the soul, buried in its own darkness, is *blind*. It is also *dumb*, not being able to confess unto salvation what it has believed unto righteousness. It is *deaf,* not hearing that living voice. It is *lame,* nay, unable to support itself, having none to whom it can say, "Thou hast held my right hand, and conducted me in thy will." In short, it performs no one function of life. For thus speaks the Prophet, when he would shew that the fountain of life is with God, (Baruch 3:14) — "Learn where there is prudence, where there is virtue, where there is understanding, where there is length of life and food, where there is light to the eyes and peace."

What more do you require for death? But, not to stop here, let us consider with ourselves what life Christ hath brought us, and then we shall understand what the death is from which he hath redeemed us. We are taught both by the Apostle, when he says,

"Awake, thou that sleepest, and arise from the dead, and Christ will give thee light." (Ephesians 5:14.)

Here it is not asses he addresses, but those who, entangled in sin, carry death and hell along with them. Again,

"You, when you were dead in sins, hath he quickened together in Christ, forgiving you all trespasses." (Ephesians 2:1.)

Accordingly, as the Apostle says, that "we die to sin," when concupiscence is extinguished in us, so we also die to God when we become subject to concupiscence living in us. (Colossians 2:13; Romans 6:2.) Nay, (to comprehend in one word what he says of the widow living in pleasure,) "while living we are dead;" in other words, we are undying in regard to death. (1 Timothy 5:6.) For although the mind retains its power of perception, yet evil concupiscence is, as it were, a kind of mental stupefaction.

Then, such death as the soul endures Christ underwent on our account; for all which the prophecies promised concerning his victory over death he performed by his death. The prophets declared, "He will overthrow death for ever." Again, "I will be thy death, O death! thy devourer, O hell!" (Isaiah 15:8; Hosea 13:14.) The Apostles proclaim the accomplishment of these things, "He hath indeed destroyed death, and illumined life by the gospel." (Colossians 2) And again,

"If, by the fault of one, death reigned by one, much more shall those who have received exuberance of grace reign through life in Christ." (Romans 5:17.)

Let them, if they can, resist these passages, which are not so much words as flashes of lightning!

When they say, what we indeed admit, that death is from Adam — death, however, not as they feign, but such as we have lately shewn to be applicable to the soul — we, on the other hand, say that life is from Christ, and this they cannot deny. The whole controversy turns on a comparison between Adam and Christ. They must necessarily concede to the Apostle not only that everything which had fallen in Adam is renewed in Christ, but inasmuch as the power of grace was stronger than that of sin, so much has Christ been more powerful in restoring than Adam in destroying: for he distinctly declares that the gift is not as the sin, but is much more exuberant, not indeed by including a greater number of individuals, but by bestowing richer blessings on those whom it includes. Let them say, if they will, that it was exuberant, not by giving more abundant life, but by effacing many sins, seeing that the one sin of Adam had plunged us into ruin. I ask no more.

Again, when he elsewhere says, that "the sting of death was sin," (1 Corinthians 15:56,) how can death longer sting us, when its sting has been blunted, nay, destroyed? The whole scope of several chapters in the Epistle to the Romans is to make it manifest that sin is completely abolished so as no longer to have dominion over believers. Then, if the strength of sin is the law, what else do they, when they slay those who live in Christ, than subject them to the curse of the law from which they had been delivered? Hence the Apostle confidently declares, (Romans 8:1,) that "there is now no condemnation to those who are in Christ Jesus, who walk not after the flesh, but after the Spirit." On those whom the Apostle thus frees from all condemnation, they pronounce the severest of all sentences, "Dying, ye shall die!" Where is grace, if death still reigns among the elect of God? Sin, as the Apostle says, indeed reigned unto death, but grace reigns unto eternal life, and, overcoming sin, leaves no place for death. Therefore, as death reigned on entering by Adam, so now life reigns by Jesus Christ. And we know that

"Christ, being raised from the dead, dies no more: death shall no longer have dominion over him: For in that he died, he died unto sin once; but in that he lives, he lives unto God." (Romans 6:9.)

Here we may see how they themselves give their heresy its deathblow! When they say that "death is the punishment of sin," they at the same time imply that man, if he had not fallen, would have been immortal. What he began to be, he once was not; and what he is by punishment, he is not by nature. Then the Apostle exclaims that sin is absorbed by grace, so that it can no longer have any power over the elect of God; and hence we conclude that the elect now are such as Adam was before his sin; and as he was created inexterminable, so now have those become who have been renewed by Christ to a better nature. There is nothing at variance with this in the Apostle's declaration, (1 Corinthians 15:54,) "The word shall be accomplished, *(fiet:)* death has been swallowed up in victory," since no man can deny that the term *fiet* (shall be done) is synonymous with *implebitur* (shall be fulfilled.) That shall be fulfilled in the body which has now been begun in the soul; or rather, that which has only been begun in the soul will be fulfilled both in the soul and the body: for this common death which we all undergo, as it were by a common necessity of nature, is rather to the elect a kind of passage to the highest degree of immortality, than either an evil or a punishment, and, as Augustine says, (De Discrimine Vitae Human. et Brut., c. 43,) is nothing else than the falling off of the flesh, which does not consume the things connected with it, but divides them, seeing it restores each to its original.

Their *third* Argument is, That those who have died are in many places said to SLEEP, as in the case of Stephen, "He fell asleep in the Lord;" again, "Our Lazarus sleepeth;" again, "Be not anxious about them who are asleep." (Acts 7:60; John 11:11; 1 Thessalonians 4:13.) The same occurs so often in the books of Kings, that there is scarcely an expression which is more familiar. But the passage on which they most strenuously insist is taken from the book of Job:

"A tree has hope: if it is cut down it grows green again, and its branches bud forth, etc.; but when man has died and been laid bare and consumed, where is he? As when the waters of the sea recede, and the channel left empty becomes dry, so man when he has fallen asleep will not rise nor be awakened out of his sleep till the heavens be crushed." (Job 14:7-12.)

But if you hold that souls sleep because death is called sleeping, then the soul of Christ must have been seized with the same sleep: for David thus speaks in his name, (Psalm 3:6,) "I laid me down and slept; I rose up, for the Lord sustained me." And he hears his enemies in insult exclaiming, (Psalm 41:9,) "Will he who sleeps rise again?" But if, as has been more fully discussed, nothing so mean and abject is to be imagined in regard to the soul of Christ, no man can doubt that the Scripture referred merely to the external composition of the body, and described it as sleep from so appearing to man. The two expressions are used indiscriminately, "he slept with his fathers," "he was laid with his fathers" — although no man's soul is laid with the soul of his fathers when his body is carried to their tomb. In the same sense, I think this sleep is attributed to impious kings, in the books of Kings and Chronicles.

When you hear that the wicked man sleeps, do you think of a sleep of his soul? It cannot have a worse executioner to torment it than an evil conscience. How can there be sleep amid such anguish? "The wicked are like the tempestuous sea which cannot rest, and whose waves cast up mire and dirt.

"There is no peace to the wicked, saith the Lord." (Isaiah 57:21.)

And yet, when David wished to describe the bitterest pang of conscience, he says, (Psalm 13:4) "Enlighten my eyes, lest I sleep the sleep of death." The jaws of hell yawn to engulf him, the power of sin tosses him about, and yet he sleeps, nay, sleeps just because he so suffers! Here, too, we must send those back to their rudiments who have not yet learned that by synecdoche the whole is sometimes taken for a part, and sometimes a part for the whole — a figure which is constantly occurring in Scripture. I do not wish the fact to be taken on my word, but. will produce passages to prove it. When Job said,

"Behold I now sleep in the dust, and if ye seek me in the morning I shall not subsist," (Job 7:21,)

did he think that his soul was to be overwhelmed with sleep? His soul was not to be thrown into the dust, and therefore was not to sleep in the dust. When he said in another passage,

"And yet they shall sleep in the dust, and the worms shall cover them," (Job 21:26)

and when David said,

"Like the wounded sleeping in their tombs," (Psalm 88:6,)

do you think that they put souls down before worms to be gnawed by them?

To the same effect the Prophet, when describing the future destruction of Nebuchadnezzar says,

"The whole land has rested and been silent, the fir-trees also and the cedars of Lebanon have rejoiced over thee; from the time at which thou didst fall asleep, no one has come up to hew us down." (Isaiah 14:8.)

A little after he says,

"All the kings of the nations have slept in glory, each man in his place, but thou hast been cast forth from the tomb." (Isaiah 14:18, 19.)

All these things were said of a dead body, "sleeping," being used as equivalent to lying or being stretched out, as sleepers do when stretched on the ground. This mode of expression might be taught us by profane writers, one of whom says, "When once our short light has set, an everlasting night must be slept ;" and another, "Fool, what is sleep?" and again:, "Let the bones of Naso lie softly." These expressions are used by writers who have many monstrous fictions respecting the lower regions, and describe the many and various feelings by which the shades of the dead are affected, Hence the very name given by the ancients to places destined for sepulture was koimhthrion, ("cemetery," or "sleepingplace.") They did not imagine that dead souls were then laid to rest, but spoke only of the body. I presume that I have now sufficiently disposed of the smoke in which they involved their "Sleep of the Soul," by proving that nowhere in Scripture is the term sleep applied to the soul, when it is used to designate death. We have elsewhere discoursed fully of "The Rest of the Soul."

The *fourth* Argument which they urge against us, as their most powerful battering ram, is the passage in which Solomon thus writes in his Ecclesiastes, (Ecclesiastes 3:18-21,) "I said in my heart of the children of men that God would prove them to show that they were like the brutes. As man dies, so do they also die. In like manner all things breathe, and man has no more than a beast of burden. All things are subject to vanity, and hasten to one place. Of earth have they been made, and to earth do they equally return. Who knows whether the spirit of the sons of Adam ascends upwards, and the spirit of beasts descends downwards?"

What if Solomon himself here answers them in one word? "Vanity of vanities, saith the Preacher, vanity of vanities, and all is vanity!" For what else does he aim at than to show the vain sense of man, and the uncertainty of all things? Man sees that he dies like the brutes, that he has life and death in common with them; and he therefore infers that his condition is on an equality with theirs: and as nothing remains to them after death, so he makes nothing remain to himself. This is the mind of man, this his reason, this his intellect!

"For the animal man receiveth not the things of the Spirit; they are foolishness unto him, neither can he understand them." (1 Corinthians 2:14.)

Man looks with the eyes of flesh and beholds death present, and the only reflection he makes is, that all things have sprung from the earth, and equally return to the earth; meanwhile, he takes no account of the soul. And this is the meaning of the subjoined clause, "Who knows whether the spirit of the sons of Adam ascends upwards?" For if the subject of the soul is considered, human nature, wholly contracted in itself, comprehends nothing distinctly or clearly by studying, meditating, and reasoning.

Therefore, when Solomon shows the vanity of human sense, from the consideration, that in examining the mind, it fluctuates and is held in suspense, he by no means countenances their error, but; nobly supports our faith. That which exceeds the capacity and little measure of the human mind, the wisdom of God explains, assuring us that the spirit of the sons of Adam ascends upwards. I will bring forward a similar passage from the same writer for the purpose of somewhat bending their stubborn neck.

"Man does not understand either the hatred or the love of God towards men, but all things are kept uncertain, because all things happen equally to the righteous and the wicked, the good and bad, to him sacrificing victims and to him not sacrificing." (Ecclesiastes 9:1.)

If all things are kept uncertain in regard to the future, shall the believer, to whom all things work together for good, regard affliction as an evidence of divine hatred? By no means. For believers have been told, "In the world you shall have tribulation — in me, consolation." Supported by this consideration, they not only endure whatever befalls them with unshaken magnanimity, but even glory in tribulation, acknowledging with blessed Job, "Though he slay us, we will hope in him." (Job 13:15.)

How, then, are all things kept uncertain in regard to the future? This is only humanly speaking. But every living man is vanity. He adds,

"The worst thing I have seen under the sun is, that the same things happen to all; hence the hearts of the children of men are filled with malice and contempt in their life, and afterwards are taken down to the lower regions. There is no man who can live always, or have expectation of such a thing. A living dog is better than a dead lion. For the living know that they shall die, but the dead no longer know anything. Nor have they further any Reward; for their memory is given up to oblivion," etc. (Ecclesiastes 9:3-5.)

Does he not speak thus of the gross stupidity of those who see only what is actually present, hoping neither for Future Life nor Resurrection? For even if it were true that we are nothing after death, still the Resurrection remains; and, would they fix their hopes on it, they would neither feel contempt for God, nor be filled with all kinds of wickedness, not to mention other things. Let us therefore conclude, with Solomon, that all these things are beyond the reach of human reason. But if we would have any certainty, let us run to the law and the testimony, where are the truth and the ways of the Lord. They declare to us —

"Until the dust return to the earth whence it was, and the spirit return to God who gave it." (Ecclesiastes 12:7.)

Let no one, then, who has heard the word of the Lord, have any doubt that the spirit of the children of Adam ascends upwards. By "ascending upwards" in that passage, I understand simply subsisting and retaining immortality, just as "descending downwards" seems to me to mean lapsing, falling, becoming lost.

Their *fifth* Argument they thunder forth with so much noise, that it might arouse the sleeping out of the deepest sleep. They place their greatest hope of victory in it, and, when they would gloss over matters to their neophytes, place most dependence upon it as a means of shaking their faith and overcoming their good sense. There is one judgment, they say, which will render to all their reward — to the pious, glory — to the impious, hell-fire. No blessedness or misery is fixed before that day. This the Scriptures uniformly declare —

"He will send his angels with a trumpet and a loud voice, and they will assemble his elect from the four winds, from the heights of heaven to the utmost limits thereof." (Matthew 24:31.)

Again,

"At the end of the world, the Son of man will send his angels, and they will gather out of his kingdom all things that offend, and those who do iniquity, and will send them into the furnace of fire. Then the righteous will shine forth like the sun in the kingdom of their Father." (Matthew 13:41.)

Again,

"Then will the King say to them on his right hand, Come, ye blessed of my Father, inherit the kingdom prepared for you from the foundation of the world." "Depart from me, ye cursed, into everlasting fire." "And they shall go away, the latter to eternal punishment, and the former to eternal life." (Matthew 25:34.)

To the same effect is the passage in Daniel 12,

"And in that time shall thy people be saved, all of them whose names shall be found written in the book."

They ask, If all these things have been written of the day of judgment, how will the elect be then called to the possession of the heavenly kingdom, if they already possess it? How can they be told to come, if they are already there? How will the people be then saved if they are safe now? Wherefore believers, who even now walk in faith, do not expect any other day of salvation, as Paul says, (2 Corinthians 4:14,)

"Knowing that he who raised up Jesus from the dead will also raise us up with Jesus."

And elsewhere, "Waiting for the revelation of our Lord Jesus Christ, who will confirm us even unto the end, against the day of his approach," etc.

But though we were to concede all these things to them, why do they make their own addition about "sleep?" For in all these, and similar passages, they cannot produce one syllable concerning sleep. Though they be awake, they may be without glory. Wherefore, since it is the part of a senseless, not to say presumptuous man, to decide peremptorily, without any authority from Scripture, on points which do not fall under human sense, with what countenance do those new and swollen dogmatists proceed to maintain a sleep of which they have heard nothing from the lips of our Lord? All persons of sense and soberness may hence see that a sleep which cannot be proved from the plain word of God is a wicked fiction. But let us take up the passages in order, lest the more simple be moved when they hear that the salvation of souls is deferred to the day of judgment.

First, we wish it to be held as an acknowledged point, as we have already explained, That our blessedness is always in progress up to that day which shall conclude and terminate all progress, and that thus the glory of the elect, and complete consummation of hope, look forward to that day for their fulfillment. For it is admitted by all, that perfection of blessedness or glory nowhere exists except in perfect union with God. Hither we all tend, hither we hasten, hither all the Scriptures and the divine promises send us. For that which was once said to Abraham applies to us also, (Genesis 15:1,) "Abraham, I am thy exceeding great reward." Seeing, then, that the reward appointed for all who have part with Abraham is to possess God and enjoy him, and that, besides and beyond it, it is not lawful to long for any other, thither must our eyes be turned when the subject of our expectation is considered. Thus far, if I mistake not, our opponents are agreed with us. On the other hand, I hope they will concede that that kingdom, to the possession of which we are called, and which is elsewhere denominated "salvation," and "reward," and "glory," is nothing else than that union with God by which they are fully in God, are filled by God, in their turn cleave to God, completely possess God — in short, are "one with God." For thus, while they are in the fountain of all fullness, they reach the ultimate goal of righteousness, wisdom, and glory, these being the blessings in which the kingdom of glory consists. For Paul intimates that the kingdom of God is in its highest perfection when "God is all in all." (1 Corinthians 15:28.) Since on that day, only God will be all in all, and completely fill his believers, it is called, not without reason, "the day of our salvation," before which our salvation is not perfected in all its parts. For those whom God fills are filled with riches which neither ear can hear, nor eye see, nor tongue tell, nor imagination conceive.

If these two points are beyond controversy, our hypnologists (sleepmaintainers) in vain endeavor to prove that the holy servants of God, on departing this life, do not yet enter the kingdom of God, from its being said, "Come" — "inherit the kingdom"— and so forth. For it is easy for us to answer that it does not follow that there is no kingdom because there is not a perfect one; on the contrary, we maintain that that which has been already begun is then to be perfected. This I only wish to be conceded to me when I shall have made it plain by sure Scripture argument.

That day is called "the kingdom of God," because he will then make adverse powers truly subject, slay Satan by the breath of his mouth, and destroy him by the brightness of his coming, while he himself will wholly dwell and reign in his elect. (1 Corinthians 15:24; 2 Thessalonians 2:8.) God in himself cannot reign otherwise than he reigned from the beginning. Of his majesty there cannot be increase or diminution. But it is called "His kingdom," because it will be manifested to all. When we pray that his kingdom may come, do we imagine that previously it exists not? And when will it be? "The kingdom of God is within you." (Luke 17:21) God, therefore, now reigns in his elect whom he guides by his Spirit. He reigns also in opposition to the devil, sin, and death, when he bids the light, by which error and falsehood are confounded, to shine out of darkness, and when he prohibits the powers of darkness from hurting those who have the mark of the Lamb in their foreheads. He reigns, I say, even now, when we pray that his kingdom may come. He reigns, indeed, while he performs miracles in his servants, and gives the law to Satan. But his kingdom will properly come when it will be completed. And it will be completed when he will plainly manifest the glory of his majesty to his elect for salvation, and to the reprobate for confusion.

And what else is to be said or believed of the elect, whose kingdom and glory it is to be in the glorious kingdom of God, and as it were reign with God and glory in him — in short, to be partakers of the Divine glory? This kingdom, though it is said not yet to have come, may yet be in some measure beheld. For those who in a manner have the kingdom of God within them, and reign with God, begin to be in the kingdom of God; the gates of hell cannot prevail against them. They are justified in God, it being said of them,

"In the Lord will all the seed of Israel be justified and praised." (Isaiah 45:25.)

That kingdom wholly consists in the building up of the Church, or the progress of believers, who, as described to us by Paul, (Ephesians 4:13,)grow up, through all the different stages of life, into "a perfect man."

These good folks see the beginnings of this kingdom — see the increase. As soon as these disappear from their eyes, they give no place to faith, and are unable to believe what the eye of flesh has ceased to behold. Very different is the conduct of the Apostle! He says,

"Ye are dead, and your life is hid with Christ in God. When Christ your life shall appear, then shall ye also appear with him in glory." (Colossians 3:4.)

He indeed attributes to us a hidden life with Christ our Head beside God; he delays the glory to the day of the glory of Christ, who, as the Head of the Church, will bring his members with him. The very same thing is expressed by John, though in different terms, —

"Beloved, now are we the sons of God; but it hath not yet appeared what we shall be: but we know that when he shall appear, we shall be like him, since we shall see him as he is." (1 John 3:2.)

He says not that meanwhile, for some length of time, we shall be nothing; but, seeing we are the sons of God, who wait for the inheritance of the Father, he keeps up and suspends our expectation, till that day on which the glory of Christ will be manifest in all, and we shall be glorified in him. Here, again, we cannot help wondering that, when they hear of "sons of God," they do not return to a sound mind, and perceive that this is an immortal generation which is of God, and by which we are partakers of a Divine immortality. But to proceed —

Let them cry out, as much as they please, that they are not called the blessed of God before the day of judgment, and that not before it is salvation promised to the people of God. I answer, that Christ is our Head, whose kingdom and glory have not yet appeared: if the members precede, the order is perverted and preposterous. We shall follow our Prince when he shall come in the glory of his Father, and sit in the seat of his majesty. Meanwhile, there is life in all within us that is of God — that is, our spirit, because Christ our life lives. For it were absurd to say we perish, while our life is living! This life is both beside God and with God, and is blessed because it is in God. All these things are self-evident, and in accordance with the truth. Why are those who have died in the Lord said to be not yet saved, or not yet to possess the kingdom of God? Because they wait for what they as yet have not, and have not reached the summit of their felicity. Why are they, nevertheless, happy? Because they both perceive God to be propitious to them, and see their future reward from a distance, and rest in the sure hope of a blessed Resurrection. As long as we dwell in this prison of clay, we hope for what we see not, and against hope believe in hope, as the Apostle says of Abraham. (Romans 4:18.) But when the eyes of our mind, now dull because buried in flesh, shall have thrown off this dullness, we shall see what we waited for, and be delighted in that rest. We are not afraid to speak thus, after the Apostle, who says conversely, that a fearful looking for of judgment awaits the reprobate. (Hebrews 10:27.) If this is called "fearful," the other surely may be justly called "joyful" and "blessed."

Since it is more my purpose to instruct than to crush my opponents, let them lend me their ear for a little, while we extract the reality from a figure of the Old Testament, and that not without authority. As Paul, in speaking of the passage of the Israelites across the Red Sea, allegorically represents the drowning of Pharaoh as the mode of deliverance by water, (1 Corinthians 10:1,) so we may be permitted to say that in baptism our Pharaoh is drowned, our old man is crucified, our members are mortified, we are buried with Christ., and remove from the captivity of the devil and the power of death, but remove only into the desert, a land arid and poor, unless the Lord rain manna from heaven, and cause water to gush forth from the rock. For our soul, like that land without water, is in want of all things, till he, by the grace of his Spirit, rain upon it. We afterwards pass into the land of promise, under the guidance of Joshua the son of Nun, into a land flowing with milk and honey; that is, the grace of God frees us from the body of death, by our Lord Jesus

Christ, not without sweat and blood, since the flesh is then most repugnant, and exerts its utmost force in warring against the Spirit. After we take up our residence in the land, we feed abundantly. White robes and rest are given us. But Jerusalem, the capital and seat of the kingdom, has not yet been erected; nor yet does Solomon, the Prince of Peace, hold the scepter and rule over all.

The souls of the saints, therefore, which have escaped the hands of the enemy, are after death in peace. They are amply supplied with all things, for it is said of them, "They shall go from abundance to abundance." But when the heavenly Jerusalem shall have risen up in its glory, and Christ, the true Solomon, the Prince of Peace, shall be seated aloft on his tribunal, the true Israelites will reign with their King. Or — if you choose to borrow a similitude from the affairs of men — we are fighting with the enemy, so long as we have our contest with flesh and blood; we conquer the enemy when we put off the body of sin, and become wholly God's; we will celebrate our triumph, and enjoy the fruits of victory, when our head shall be raised above death in glow, that is, when death shall be swallowed up in victory. This is our aim, this our goal; and of this it has been written,

"I shall be satisfied when I awake with beholding thy glory." (Psalm 17:15.)

These things may be easily learned Scripture, by all who have learned to hear God and hearken to his voice.

The same things have been handed down to us by tradition, from those who have cautiously and reverently handled the mysteries of God. For ancient writers, while declaring that souls are indeed in paradise, and in heaven, have not hesitated to say that they have not yet received their glory and reward. Tertullian says, (Lib. de Resurrect. Carnis,) "Both the reward and the peril depend on the event of the Resurrection." And yet he teaches, without any ambiguity, that "previously to that event souls are with God, and live in God." In another place he says, "Why do we not comprehend that by Abraham's bosom is meant a temporary receptacle of faithful souls, wherein the image of faith is delineated, and a clear view of both judgments exhibited?" The words of Irenaeus (Lib. 9, adv. Haeres.) are, "Since our Lord departed, in the midst of the shadow of death, to the place where the souls of the dead were, thereafter rose again bodily, and after his Resurrection was taken up, it is manifest, both that the souls of his disciples, on whose account the Lord performed these things, will go away into the invisible place assigned them by the Lord, and there remain until the Resurrection, waiting for the Resurrection; afterwards recovering their bodies, and rising again perfectly, that is, bodily, as the Lord also rose, they will come into the presence of God. 'For the disciple is not above his Master,'" etc.

Chrysostom says, (Hom. 28, in 11 ad Hebr.,) "Understand what and how great a thing it is for Abraham to sit and the Apostle Paul, when he is perfected, that they may then be able to receive their reward. Unless we come thither the Father hath foretold us that he will not give the reward, as a good father who loves his children says to probable children and those finishing their labor, that he will not give food till the other brothers have come. Are you anxious because you do not yet receive? What then will Abel do, who formerly conquered, and still sits without a crown? What will Noah do? What the others of those times? Lo! they have waited and still wait for others who are to be after thee." A little after he says, "They were before us in the contest, but they will not be before us in the crown; for there is one set time for all the crowns."

Augustine, in many passages, describes the secret receptacles in which the souls of the righteous are kept until they receive the crown and the glory, while meanwhile the reprobate suffer punishment, waiting for the precise measure to be fixed by the judgment. (De Civitate, Lib. 12 c. 9; Lib. 13 c. 8, et alibi.) And in an Epistle to Jerome he says, "The soul after the death of the body will have rest, and will at length receive the body into glory." Bernard, professedly handling this question in two sermons delivered on the Feast of All Saints, teaches, that "the souls of the saints, divested of their bodies, still stand in the courts of the Lord, admitted to rest but not yet to glory. Into that most blessed abode," he says, "they shall neither enter without us, nor without their own bodies;" that is, neither saints without other believers, nor spirits without flesh: and many other things to the same purpose.

Those who place them in heaven, provided they do not attribute to them the glory of the Resurrection, do not differ from that view. This Augustine himself, in another place, apparently does. (De Ecclesiastes Dogmat.) For while it is certain that wicked demons are now tormented, (as Peter affirms, 2 Peter 2;) yet that fire into which the reprobate will be sent on the day of judgment, is said here to be prepared for the devil. (Jude.) Both things are expressed when it is said, that they are "reserved in eternal chains against the judgment of the great day;" — "reserved" here intimating the punishment which they as yet feel not, and "chains" the punishment which they actually endure. And Augustine explains himself in another passage, (in Psalm 36.) where he says, "Assuredly your last day cannot be far distant. Prepare yourself for it. Such as you depart this life, such will you be restored to that life. After that life you shall not instantly be where the saints will be, to whom it will be said, 'Come, ye blessed of my Father, inherit the kingdom which was prepared for you from the foundation of the world.' That you shall not yet be there every one knows; but you shall be where the proud and niggardly rich man in the midst of his torments saw the poor beggar, who was formerly covered with sores, resting far away. Placed in that rest you will wait secure against the day of judgment, when you will recover your body, when you will be changed and made like the angels."

Nor do I object to the illustration which he elsewhere gives, (De Quantitat. Animae,) provided a sound and moderate interpretation be given to it, viz., that "there are many states of soul, *first,* animation; *second,* sense; *third,* art; *fourth,* virtue; *fifth,* tranquillity; *sixth,* ingress; *seventh,* contemplation: or, if you rather choose it, *first,* of the body; *second,* to the body; *third,* about the body; *fourth,* to itself; *fifth,* in itself; *sixth,* to God; *seventh,* with God." I have been induced to quote these words of the holy writer, rather to show what his views were, than with the idea of binding any one, or even myself, to adopt these distinctions. Even Augustine himself, I think, did not wish this, but was desirous, though in the plainest manner possible, to explain the progress of the soul: showing how it does not reach its final perfection until the day of judgment. It, moreover, occurred to me, that those who so much insist on this day of judgment may by means of it be convinced of their error. For in the Creed, which is the Compendium of our Faith, we confess the Resurrection, not of the soul, but of the body. There is no room for the cavil, that by "body" is meant the whole man. We admit; that it sometimes has this signification, but we cannot admit it here, where significant and simple expressions are used, in accommodation to the illiterate. Certainly the Pharisees, strong asserters of the Resurrection, and constantly having the term in their mouths, at the same time believed it was not spirit.

Still, however, they insist, and keep us to the point, quoting the words in which Paul declares that

"we are of all men the most miserable" if the dead rise not. (1 Corinthians 15:19)

What need is there of the Resurrection, they ask, if we are happy before the Resurrection? Nay, where is the great misery of Christians, a misery surpassing that which all others suffer, if it is true that they are in rest while others are afflicted and strongly tortured, Here I must tell them, that if I had any desire to evade the difficulty, (a thing on which they are always intent,) I have here ample opportunity. For what hinders us from adopting the view taken by some sensible Expositors, who understand the words to be spoken not only of the final Resurrection, by which we shall recover our bodies from corruption, incorruptible; but of the life which remains to us after our mortal life is over, and which is frequently designated in Scripture by the name of Resurrection? For when it is said that the Sadducees deny the Resurrection, it is not the body that is referred to, but the simple meaning is, that, according to their opinion, nothing of man survives death.

This view is made probable by the fact, that all the grounds on which the Apostle founds his statement might have been obviated by answering, that the soul indeed lives, but that the body, when once it has mouldered into dust, cannot possibly be raised. Let us furnish specimens. When he says, "Those who have fallen asleep in Christ have perished," he might have been refuted by the philosophers who strenuously asserted the immortality of the soul. When he asks, "What will those do who are baptized for the dead?" he might easily have been answered, that souls survive death. To the question, "Why are we in jeopardy every hour?" the reply might have been, that we expose this frail life for the immortality in which our better part will live.

We have now said much for which there would have been no occasion among persons of teachable disposition. For the Apostle himself says, that we are miserable if we have hope in Christ in this life only. This is clear beyond dispute, even he being witness, who acknowledges that his feet were almost gone, and that this steps had well-nigh slipped when he saw sinners enjoying themselves on the earth. And certainly, if we look only to the present, we will call those happy to whom everything turns out to a wish. But if we extend our views farther, we see that happy is the people whose God is the Lord, for in His hands are the issues of death.

We can adduce something still more decided, not only to refute their objections:, but to explain the genuine meaning of the Apostle to these who are willing to learn without being disputatious. For if there is no Resurrection of the flesh, he justly for this one reason calls the pious unhappy, because they endure so many wounds, scourges, torments, contumely, in short, necessities of all kinds in their bodies, which they think destined to immortality; seeing they will be disappointed in this their expectation. For what can be, I do not say "more miserable," but even more ridiculous, than to see the bodies of those who live for the day indulging in all kinds of delicacies, while the bodies of Christians are worn out with hunger, cold, stripes, and all kinds of contumely, if the bodies of both equally perish! I might compare this by the words which follow, "Why are we in jeopardy every hour, I die daily through your glory, brethren," etc. "Let us eat and drink, for tomorrow we die." It were better, he says, to act on the maxim, "Let us eat," etc., if the affronts which we suffer in our bodies are not compensated by that glory for which we hope! This cannot be unless by the Resurrection of the flesh. Then, though this were given up, I can adduce another argument, viz., We are more miserable than all men if there is no Resurrection, because, although we are happy before the Resurrection, we are not happy without the Resurrection. For we say that the spirits of saints are happy in this, that they rest in the hope of a blessed Resurrection, which they could not do, were all this blessedness to perish. True, there is the declaration of Paul, that we are more miserable than all men if there is no Resurrection; and there is no repugnance in these words to the dogma, that the spirits of the just are blessed before the Resurrection, since it is because of the Resurrection.

They also bring forward what is said in the Epistle to the Hebrews concerning the ancient Patriarchs, (Hebrews 11:13) "All these died in faith, not having received the promises, but seeing them afar off, because they were strangers and pilgrims on the earth. For them who say so show that they seek a country. And, indeed, had they remembered the country from which they came, they had opportunity of returning, but now they desire a better, that is, a heavenly country." Here our opponents argue as follows: If they desire a heavenly country, they do not already possess it: We, on the contrary, argue; If they desire, they must exist, for there cannot be desire without a subject in which it resides. And, as I attempt to force from them only, there must be a sense of good and evil where there is desire which either follows what carries an appearance of good, or shows that which appears evil. That desire, they say, lies in God, than which nothing can be imagined more ridiculous. For one of two things must follow — either that God desires something better than he has, or that there is something in God which belongs not to God. This circumstance makes me suppose that they are merely sporting with a serious matter.

To omit this, What is meant by "the power of returning?" Let them, then, return to a sound mind and listen to something better than they have yet embraced; if, indeed, they are really persuaded of that which they profess with their lips. The Apostle is speaking of Abraham and his posterity who dwelt in a foreign land among strangers; only not exiles, but certainly sojourners, scarcely sheltering their bodies by living in poor huts, in obedience to the command of God given to Abraham, that he should leave his land and his kindred. God had promised them what he had not yet exhibited. Therefore they trusted the promises afar off, and died in the firm belief that the promises of

God would one day be fulfilled. In accordance with this belief, they confessed that they had no fixed abode on the earth, and that beyond the earth there was a country for which they longed, viz., heaven. In the end of the chapter he intimates, that all those whom he enumerated did not obtain the final promise, that they might not be perfected without us. Had they attended to the peculiar meaning of this expression, they never would have excited so much disturbance. It is strange how they can be blind in so much light; but still more strange that they give us bread instead of stones — in other words, support our views while seeking to overthrow them!

They think they derive strong support from what is said in the Acts of the Apostles concerning Tabitha, who, when a disciple of Christ, full of alms and good deeds, was raised from the dead by Peter. (Acts 9:40.) They say, an injury was done to Tabitha, if we are correct in holding that the soul, when freed from the body, lives with God and in God, since she was brought back from the society of God and a life of blessedness to this evil world. As if the same thing might not be retorted upon them! For whether she slept, or was nothing, yet as she had died in the Lord she was blessed. It was, therefore, not expedient for her to return to the life which she had finished. They must themselves, therefore, first untie the knot which they have made, since it is but fair that they obey the law which they lay upon others. And yet it is easy for us to untie it.

Whatever be the lot which awaits us after death, what Paul says of himself, (Philippians 1:23,) is applicable to all believers — "for us to die is gain, and to be with Christ is better." And yet Paul says that Epaphroditus, who certainly was in the number of believers, "obtained mercy of the Lord when sick nigh unto death," he recovered. (Philippians 2:27.) Those men, indeed, who handle the mysteries of God with so little reverence and sobriety, would interpret that mercy as cruelty. We, however, feel and acknowledge it to be mercy, seeing it is a step of Divine mercy to sanctify the elect and glorify the sanctified. Does not the Lord then display his mercy when he sanctifies us more and more? What! if the will of God is to be magnified in our body by life, as Paul says, is it not mercy? It is not surely ours to lay down laws for the miraculous works of God; it is enough if the glory of their author shine forth in them. What if we should say that God did not consult the advantage of Tabitha, but had respect to the poor at whose prayers she was raised up, while they kept weeping and showing the garments which Tabitha was wont to sew for them? Paul thought that this mode of living sufficed him, though it were far better for him to depart to God. After saying that God had had mercy on Epaphroditus, he adds, "And not on him only, but on me also, that I might not have sorrow upon sorrow." Go now and raise a plea against God for having given back to the poor a woman who was diligent in supplying their wants! For, however the operation may appear to us, Christ, who died and rose again, that he might rule over the living and the dead, is certainly entitled to be glorified both in our life and in our death.

David also, the best defender of our cause, they call in as a defender of theirs, but with so much effrontery, and in a manner so devoid of common sense, that one is both ashamed and pained to mention the arguments which they borrow from him. The whole, however, with which we are acquainted we shall now honestly state. *First,* they venture to quote the words, (Psalm 82:6,) "I said, Ye are gods, and all of you exalted sons, but ye shall die like men," etc. And they interpret that believers are indeed gods and sons of God, but that they die and fall with the reprobate, so that there is the same lot to both till the lambs shall be separated from the kids. We give the answer which we have received from Christ, (John 10:34,) that "they are there called gods to whom the word of God came;" that is, ministers of God, namely, judges who bear in their hands the sword which they have received from God. Even had we not the interpretation of Christ and the usage of Scripture, which everywhere concurs, there is no obscurity in the passage itself, in which those are rebuked who judge iniquity and respect the faces of sinners. They are called gods, because acting as the representatives of God while they preside over others; but they are reminded of a future Judge to whom they must give an account of their office. See a specimen of the way in which our opponents argue!

Let us attend to another. It is said, *secondly,* (Psalm 146:4,) "His spirit will go forth and return to its earth. In that day all their thoughts perish." Here they take "spirit" for *wind,* and say, that the man will go away into the earth; that there will be nothing but earth; that all his thoughts will perish; whereas if there were any life they would remain. We are not so subtle, but in our dull way call a boat, a boat, and spirit, spirit! When this spirit departs from man, the man returns to the ground out of which he was taken, as we have fully explained. It remains, therefore, to see what is meant by thoughts "perishing." We are admonished not to put trust in men. Trust ought to be immortal. It were otherwise uncertain and unstable, seeing that the life of man passes quickly away. To intimate this, he said, that "their thoughts perish ;" that is, that whatever they designed while alive is dissipated and given to the winds. Elsewhere he says, "The sinner will see and be angry; he will gnash with his teeth and pine away; the desire of the sinner will perish," as it is said in another place, "dissipated:" "The Lord dissipates the counsels of the heathen:" again, "Form a scheme and it will be dissipated." The same thing, in the form of a circumlocution, is expressed by the blessed Virgin in her song, "He hath dispersed the proud in the imagination of their hearts." (Psalm 112:10; 32:10; Isaiah 8:10; Luke 1:51.)

A *third* passage which they adduce is, (Psalm 78:39,) "And he remembered that they are flesh, the spirit going and not returning." They here contend, as they uniformly do, that "spirit" is used for wind. In this they perceive not that they not only destroy the immortality of the soul, but also cut off all hope of Resurrection. For if there is a resurrection, the spirit certainly returns; and if it does not return, there is no Resurrection! Wherefore, they ought here rather to implore pardon for their imprudence than insist on such a concession being made to them. Thus much I have said merely to let all men see how easily I might be quit were it my only object to refute their arguments. For we willingly admit, in accordance with their assertion, that the term *wind* is here applicable. We grant that men are "a wind which flies and returns not:" but if they wrest this to their own views, they err, not knowing the Scriptures, with which it is common by that kind of circumlocution to intimate at one time the weakness of man's condition, at another the shortness of life.

When Job says of man, (Job 14:1,) "He is a flower which cometh forth, and is cut down, and fleeth as a shadow," what more did he mean than just to say that man is fleeting, and frail, and like a fading flower? Isaiah again is ordered to exclaim,

"All flesh is grass, and all the glory of man as the flower of the grass; the grass withereth, and the flower thereof hath fallen away; but the word of the Lord endureth for ever." (Isaiah 40:6.)

Here let them infer, in one word, that the soul of man withers and pines away, and see a little more acutely than the dull fisherman who proves from it that all believers are immortal, because born again of incorruptible seed — that is, the word of God, which endureth for ever. Scripture gives the name of "fading flower" and "passing wind" to those who put their trust in this life. Having here as it were fixed their permanent abode, they think they are to reign without end; not looking to the end by which their condition is to be changed, and they must go elsewhere. Of such persons the Prophet also says, (Isaiah 28:15,) "We have stipulated with death, and made a compact with hell."

Deriding their vain hope, he does not account as life that which is to them the beginning of the worst death. And he affirms that they cease and die, since it were better for them not to be than be what they are.

To the same effect we read in another Psalm,

"As a father pitieth his children, so the Lord pitieth all that fear him. For he knoweth our frame, he remembereth that we are dust. And man is as grass, his day is a flower of the field, so will he flourish. For his spirit will pass away in him, and he will not subsist, and he shall no longer know his place." (Psalm 103:13.)

If they affirm from these verses that the spirit perishes and vanishes away, I again warn them not to open a door for atheists, if there are any such, to rise up and endeavor to overthrow their faith and ours in the Resurrection, as there are certainly many. For in the same way they will infer that the spirit does not return to the body, seeing it is said that it shall no longer know its place. They may say, the inference is erroneous, since such arguing is plainly in the face of the passages relating to the Resurrection; but I rejoice that their inference also is erroneous, since the mode of arguing is common to both.

Almost similar to this is the passage in Ecclesiasticus, "The number of the years of man, as much as a hundred years, have been counted as the drop of water in the sea, and as the sand on the sea shore; but they are few compared with the whole duration of time. Therefore God is patient towards them, and sheds out his mercy upon them." (Ecclesiasticus 18:8- 10.) Here they must admit that the prophet's sentiment was very different; from that which they dream, and means that the Lord pitied those whom he knew to stand by his mercy alone, and, who, were he for a little to withdraw his hand, would return to the dust whence they were taken. Thereafter he subjoins a brief description of human life, comparing it to a flower which, though it blooms today, will be nothing more than dead herbage tomorrow.

Had he even declared that the spirit of man perishes and comes to nothing, he would not have given any defence to their error. For when we say that the spirit of man is immortal, we do not affirm that it can stand against the hand of God, or subsist without his agency. Far from us be such blasphemy! But we say that it is sustained by his hand and blessing. Thus Irenaeus, who with us asserts the immortality of the spirit, (Irenaeus adv. Haeres. lib. 5,) wishes us, however, to learn that by nature we are mortal, and God alone immortal. And in the same place he says, "Let us not be inflated and raise ourselves up against God, as if we had life of ourselves; and let us learn by experience that we have endurance for eternity through his goodness, and not from our nature." Our whole controversy with David then, whom they insist on making our opponent, is simply this — He says, (Psalm 39:11,) that man, if the Lord withdraw his mercy from him, falls away and perishes; we teach, that he is supported by the kindness and power of God, since he alone has immortality, and that whatever life exists is from him.

A *fourth* passage which they produce is,

"My soul is filled with evil, and my life has drawn near to hell. I am counted with those who go down into the deep, like a man without a helper, like the slain sleeping in their tombs, of whom thou art no longer mindful, they having been cut off from thy hand." (Psalm 88:4.)

What! they ask, if they have been cut off from the energy of God, if they have fallen away from his care and remembrance, have they not ceased to be? As if I had it not in my power to retort. What! if they have been cut off from the energy of God, if they have escaped his remembrance, how will they ever again be? And when will the Resurrection be? Again, how do the things agree? "The souls of the just are in the hands of God," (Wisdom 3:1;) or, to quote only from the sure oracles of God,

"The just will be in eternal remembrance." (Psalm 112:6.)

They have not therefore fallen from the hand of the Lord, nor escaped his remembrance. Nay, rather, in this mode of expression, let us perceive the deep feelings of an afflicted man, who complains before God that he is almost abandoned with the wicked to perdition, whom God is said not to know and to have forgotten; because their names are not written in the book of life; and to have been cut away from his hand:, because he does not guide them by his Spirit.

The *fifth* passage is, (Psalm 88:11,)

"Wilt thou do wonders to the dead, or will physicians raise them up, and they will confess to thee? Will any one narrate thy mercy in the tomb, or thy righteousness in the land of forgetfulness?"

Again, (Psalm 115:17,)

"The dead will not praise thee, O Lord, nor all who descend into the lower parts; but we who live bless the Lord from this time, yea, even for ever."

Again, (Psalm 30:9,)

"What utility is there in my blood when I shall have descended into corruption? Will the dust confess to thee, or announce thy truth?"

To these passages they join another of very similar import from the song of Hezekiah, (Isaiah 38:18,)

"For the grave will not confess to thee, nor will death praise thee: those who descend into the pit will not wait for thy truth. The living, the living he will confess, to thee, as I too do today; the father will make known thy truth to his children."

They add from Ecclesiasticus, "From the dead, as being nothing, there is nothing; there is no confession. Thou the living wilt confess." (Ecclesiasticus 17:26.)

We answer, that in these passages the term "dead" is not applied simply to those who have paid the common debt of nature when they depart this life: nor is it simply said that the praises of God cease at death; but the meaning partly is, that none will sing praises to the Lord save those who have felt his goodness and mercy; and partly, that his name is not celebrated after death, because his benefits are not, there declared among men as on the earth. Let us consider all the passages, and handle them in order, so that we may give to each its proper meaning. *First,* let us learn this much, that though by death the dissolution of the present life is repeatedly signified, and by the lower region, (*infernus,*) the grave, yet it is no uncommon thing for Scripture to employ these terms for the anger and withdrawal of the power of God; so that persons are said to die and descend into the lower region, or to dwell in the lower region, when they are alienated from God, or prostrated by the judgment of God, or crushed by his hand. The lower region itself (*infernus ipse*) may signify, not the grave, but abyss and confusion. And this meaning, which occurs throughout Scripture, is most familiar in the Psalms: "Let death come upon them, and let them go down alive into the pit," (*infernum:*) Again, "O my God, be not silent, lest I become like those who go down into the pit," (*lacum:*) Again, "O Lord, thou hast brought up my soul from the lower region, (*inferno,*) and saved me from these going down into the pit," (*lacum:*) Again, "Let sinners be turned into *infernus,* and all the nations which forget God:" Again, "Had not the Lord assisted me, my soul had almost dwelt in *infernus.*" Again, "Our bones have been scattered along *infernus.*" Again, "He hath placed me in dark places, like the dead of the world." (Psalm 28:1; 53:15; 30:4; 9:18; 14:7; 143:3.)

In the New Testament, where the Evangelists use the term a||dhv, the translator has rendered it by *infernus.* Thus, it is said of the rich man, "When he was in hell," (*infernus,*) etc. (Luke 16:23.) Again, "And thou, Capernaum, shalt thou be exalted unto heaven? Verily I say unto thee, thou shalt descend even unto hell," (*infernus.*) (Matthew 11:23.) In these places it signifies not so much the locality, as the condition of those whom God has condemned and doomed to destruction. And this is the confession which we make in the Creed, viz., that Christ "descended into hell," (*in inferos;*) in other words, that He was subjected by the Father, on our account, to all the pains of death; that he endured all its agonies and terrors, and was truly afflicted, it having been previously said that "he was buried."

On the other hand, those are said to LIVE, and be about to live, whom the Lord visits in kindness: "For there the Lord hath commanded the blessing and life even for evermore." Again, "That he may deliver their souls from death, and nourish them in famine." Again, "The Lord will pluck thee up from thy tabernacle, and thy root from the land of the living." Again, "I will please the Lord in the region of the living." (Psalm 133:3; 33:19; 52:7; 56:14.)

To make a conclusion, let one passage suffice us, which so graphically depicts both conditions as fully to explain its own meaning, without our saying a word: It is in Psalm 49, "Those who confide in much strength and glory in the multitude of riches. The brother does not redeem, will man redeem? Will he not give his own atonement to God, and the price of redemption for his soul, and labor for ever, and still live even to the end? Shall he not see death, when he shall see the wise dying? The unwise and the foolish will perish together. Like sheep they have been laid in the grave, (*infernus.*) Death shall feed upon them; and the just will rule over them in the morning, and assistance will perish in the grave (infernus,) from their glory. Nevertheless God will redeem my soul from the hand of hell, (*infernus,*) when He will receive me." The sum is, those who trust in their riches and strength will die and descend into *infernus;* the rich and the poor, the foolish and the wise, will perish together: he who hopes in the Lord will be free from the power of hell, (*infernus.*)

I maintain that these names "DEATH" and "HELL," (*Mors et Infernus,*) cannot have any other meaning in the verses of the Psalms which they obtrude upon us, nor in that song of Hezekiah; and I hold that this can be proved by clear arguments: for in the verses, "Wilt thou do wonders to the dead?" etc., and "What advantage is there in my blood?" etc., either Christ the head of believers, or the Church his body speaks, shunning and deprecating *death* as something horrid and detestable. This too is done by Hezekiah in his song. Why do they shudder so at the name of *death,* if they feel God to be merciful and gracious to them? Is it because they are no more to be anything? But they will escape from this turbulent world, and instead of inimical temptations and disquietude, will have the greatest ease and blessed rest. And as they will be nothing, they will feel no evil, and will be awakened at the proper time to glory, which is neither delayed by their death, nor hastened by their life. Let us turn to the examples of other saints, and see how they felt on the subject. When Noah dies he does not deplore his wretched lot. Abraham does not lament. Jacob, even during his last breath, rejoices in waiting for the salvation of the Lord. Job sheds no tears. Moses, when informed by the Lord that his last hour is at hand, is not moved. All, as far as we can see, embrace death with a ready mind. The words in which the saints answer the call of the Lord uniformly are, "Here I am, Lord!"

There must, therefore, be something which compels Christ and his followers to such complaints. There is no doubt that Christ, when he offered himself to suffer in our stead, had to contend with the power of the devil, with the torments of hell, and the pains of death. All these things were to be done in our nature, that they might lose the right which they had in us. In this contest, therefore, when He was satisfying the rigor and severity of the Divine justice, when he was engaged with hell, death, and the devil, he entreated the Father not to abandon him in such straits, not to give him over to the power of death, asking nothing more of the Father than that our weakness, which he bore in his own body, might be freed from the power of the devil and of death. The faith on which we now lean is, that the penalty of sin committed in our nature, and which was to be paid in the same nature, in order to satisfy the Divine justice, was paid and discharged in the flesh of Christ, which was ours. Christ, therefore, does not deprecate death, but that grievous sense of the severity of God with which, on our account, he was to be seized by death. Would you know from what feeling his utterance proceeded? I cannot express it better than he himself did, in another form, when he exclaimed, "Father, Father, why hast thou forsaken me?"

Those, therefore, who are dead and buried, and carried into the land of forgetfulness, He calls "forsaken of God." In this way the saints, taught by the Spirit of God, will not use these expressions in order to avert death, when coming as the call of God, but to deprecate the judgment, anger, and severity of God, with which they feel themselves to be seized by means of death. That this may not seem an invention of my own, I ask, whether a believer would call simple natural death "the wrath and terror of God?" I do not think they will be so shameless as to affirm this. But in the same passage the Prophet thus interprets that death, (Psalm 88:7,) "Thy wrath, O God, has passed over me, and the terrors of death have troubled me." And he adds many other things applicable to the Divine anger. In another passage,

(Psalm 30:6,) the words are, "Since there is force (*momentum*) in his indignation, and life in his favor." But I exhort my readers to have recourse to the sacred volume, that from the two entire Psalms and the Song they may satisfy themselves. Thus there will be no gloss, and I feel sure of the concurrence of those who read with judgment.

We conclude, therefore, that in these passages *"death"* is equivalent to a feeling of the anger and judgment of God, and being disturbed and alarmed by this feeling. Thus Hezekiah, when he saw that he was leaving his kingdom exposed to the insult and devastation of the enemy, and leaving no offspring from which the hope of the Gentiles might descend, was filled with anxiety, by these signs of an angry and punishing God, not at the terror of death, which he afterwards overcame without any deprecation. On the whole, I acknowledge that death in itself is an evil, when it is the curse and penalty of sin, and is both itself full of terror and desolation, and drives those to despair who feel that it is inflicted on them by an angry and punishing God. The only thing which can temper the bitterness of its agonies is to know that God is our Father, and that we have Christ for our leader and companion. Those devoid of this alleviation regard death as confusion and eternal perdition, and therefore cannot praise God in their death.

The verse, *"The dead* will not praise thee,"* etc., concludes the praises of the people, when giving thanks to God for having by His hand protected them from danger. Its meaning is, Had the Lord permitted us to be oppressed, and to fall into the power of the enemy, they would have insulted His Name, and boasted that they had overcome the God of Israel; but now, when the Lord has repelled and crushed their proud spirit, when he has delivered us from their cruelty by a strong hand and uplifted arm, the Gentiles cannot ask, "Where is their God?" He hath shown himself to be truly the living God! Nor can there be any doubt of his mercy, which he has so wondrously exhibited. And here those are called "dead" and "forsaken of God," who have not felt his agency and kindness towards them, as if he had delivered up his people to the lust and ferocity of the ungodly.

This view is plainly confirmed by a speech which occurs in the Book of Baruch, or at least the book which bears his name, — " Open thine eyes and see: for not the dead who are in hell, (*infernus,*) whose spirit has been torn from their bowels, will ascribe glory and justice to God; but the soul which, sad for the magnitude of the evil, walks bent and weak, and the failing eyes and the hungry soul will give glory." (Baruch 2:17.) Here we undoubtedly see that, under the names of "dead" are included those who, afflicted and crushed by God, have gone away into destruction; and that the sad, bent, and weak soul, is that which, failing in its own strength, and having no confidence in itself, runs to the Lord, calls upon him, and from him expects assistance. Any one who will regard all these things as *prosopopoeia,* will find an easy method of explaining them, Substituting things for persons, and death for dead, the meaning will be, The Lord does not obtain praise for mercy and goodness when he afflicts, destroys, and punishes, (though the punishment, is just,) but then only creates a people for himself, who sing and celebrate the praise of his goodness, when he delivers and restores the hopes of those who were afflicted, bruised, and at despair. But lest they should cavil, and allege that we are having recourse to allegory, and figurative interpretations, I add, that the words may be taken without a figure.

I said that they act erroneously in concluding, from these passages, that *saints after death* desist from the praises of God, and that "praise" rather means *making mention* of the goodness of God, and *proclaiming* his benefits among others. The words not only admit, but necessarily require this meaning. For to announce, and narrate, and make known, as a father to his children, is not merely to have a mental conception of the

Divine glory, but is to celebrate it with the lips that others may hear. Should they here rejoin that they have it in their power to do the same thing, if (as we believe) they are with God in paradise, I answer, that to be in paradise, and live with God, is not to speak to each other, and be heard by each other, but is only to enjoy God, to feel his good will, and rest in him. If some Morpheus has revealed this to them in a dream, let them keep their certainty to themselves! I will not take part in those tortuous questions, which only foster disputation, and minister not to piety. The object of Ecclesiastes is not to show that the souls of the dead perish, but while he exhorts us early, and as we have opportunity, to confess God, he at the same time teaches that there is no time of confessing after death; that is, that there is then no time for *repentance.* If any of them still asks, What is to become of the sons of perdition? that is no matter of ours. I answer for believers, —

"They shall not die, but live, and show forth the works of the Lord." "Those who dwell in His house will praise him for ever and ever." (Psalms 118:17; 84:5.)

The *sixth* passage which they adduce is, (Psalm 144:2,) "I will praise the Lord in my life; I will sing unto my God as long as I have being." On this they argue, If he is to praise the Lord in life, and while he has being, he will not praise him after life, and when he has no being! Since I think they speak thus in mere jest and sport, I will take them up in their own humor. When Virgil's Aeneas promised gratitude to his hostess as long as memory should remain, did he intimate that he was one day to lose his memory? When he said, "While life shall animate these limbs," did he not think that he would feel grateful, even among the Manes, in those fabled plains? Far be it from us to allow them to wrest the passage, so as to fall into the heresy of Helvidius! I will now speak seriously. Lest they pretend that I have not given equal for equal, I will render fivefold:

"My God, I will confess to thee for ever:" "I will bless the Lord at all times; his praise shall always be in my mouth :" "I will confess to thee for ever, for thou didst it;" "I will praise thy name for ever and ever:" "So will I sing praise unto thy name for ever, that I may daily perform my vows." (Psalms 30:12; 34:1; 52:9; 145:1; 111:8.)

They lately claimed David as their friend! Do they now perceive how strenuously he assails them? Have done, then, with arguments which are merely framed out of garbled passages or fragments!

Their *seventh* passage is,

"Cease from me and I shall be strengthened, until I go and be no more." (Psalm 34:14)

To this they join the passage of Job,

"Send me away that I may for a little bewail my sorrow, before I go and return not; to the darksome land, a land armed with the blackness of death, a land of misery and darkness, where is the shadow of death, and no order, and where eternal horror dwells." (Job 10:20.)

All this is irrelevant. The words are full of smart and anxiety of conscience, truly expressing, and, as it were, graphically depicting the feeling of those who, smitten with the terror of the Divine judgment, are no longer able to bear the hand of God. And they pray, that if they deserve to be cast off by God, they may at least be permitted to breathe a little from the anger of God, by which they are agitated, and that under extreme despair. Nor is it strange that the holy servants of God are brought to this, for the Lord mortifies and quickens them, takes them down to the lower regions, and brings them back. The expression "not to be," is equivalent to *being estranged from God.* For if He is the only being who truly is, those truly are not who are not in him; because they are perpetually cast down and discarded from his presence. Then I see not why the mode of expression should be so offensive to them, when they are not said to be *absolutely dead,* but dead only with reference to men. For they are no longer with men, nor in the presence of men, but only with God. Thus (to explain in one word) "not to be" is *not to be visibly existing,* as expressed in the passage of Jeremiah, "A voice was heard in Ramah, Rachel weeping for her children, and would not be comforted, for they are not." (Jeremiah 31:15; Matthew 2:18.)

Let us now consider the remaining passages taken from the history of Job. We have touched on some in passing as they occurred. The first is, (Job 3:11-19,)

"Why did I not die in the womb? Why did I not perish at my birth? Why was I taken upon the knee and placed at the breast? For now, sleeping, I would be silent and rest in my sleep with the kings and rulers of the earth who build deserts for themselves, or with princes, who possess gold and fill their houses with silver, or as an abortive hidden thing would not exist, but be like those who were conceived, but never saw the light. There the wicked have ceased from turmoil, and the weary are at rest; and those once bound, freed from molestation, have not heard the voice of the oppressor. The small and the great are there, and the slave is free from his master."

What if I should retort with the 14th chapter of Isaiah, where *"the dead"* are described as coming forth from their tombs and going to meet the king of Babylon, and thus addressing him, "Lo! thou art humbled like us," etc. I would have as good ground to argue that the dead feel and understand, as they have to infer that they have lost all power of perception. But I make them welcome to all such trifling. In explaining the passage which they quote, we shall not find much difficulty, if we do not make labyrinths for ourselves. Job, when pressed with sore affliction, and in a manner borne down by the load, sees only his present misery, and makes it not only the greatest of all afflictions, but almost the only affliction. He shudders not at death, nay, he longs for it as putting all on an equal footing, as ending the tyranny of kings and the oppression of slaves, as, in short, the final goal, at which every one may lay aside the condition which has been allotted him in this life. Thus he hopes that he himself will see the end of his calamity; meanwhile, he considers not on what terms he is to live there, what he is to do, what to suffer. He only longs earnestly for a change of his present state, as is usual with those who are pressed and borne down with any grievous distress. For if, during the scorching summer's heat, we deem winter pleasant, and, on the other hand, when benumbed by the winter's cold, we wish with all our heart; for summer, what will he do who feels the hand of God opposed to him? He will recoil from no evil, provided he can escape the present one. If they are not persuaded of this, there is no wonder. They excerpt and provide themselves with minute passages, but overlook the general scope. Those who have looked distinctly at the whole narrative will, I am confident, approve my explanation.

The *second* passage is, (Job 7:7,)

"Remember that my life is wind, and my eye will not return to see good, nor will the eye of man behold me. Thy eyes are upon me, and I shall not subsist. As the cloud is consumed and passes away, so he who has gone down to the lower parts will not reascend.

In these words Job, deploring his calamity before God, exaggerates in this, that no hope of escape is mentioned. He only sees his calamities, which are pursuing him to the grave. Then it occurs to him that a miserable death will be the termination of a calamitous life. For he who feels the hand of God opposed to him cannot think otherwise. From this amplification he excites commiseration, and laments his case before God. I see not what else you can discover in this passage, unless it be that no Resurrection is to be expected — a point which this is not the place to discuss.

The *third* passage is, (Job 17:1,) "The grave alone remains for me." Again, "Everything of mine shall descend into the depths of hell," (*infernus.*) This, indeed, is most true. For nothing better remains for him who has not God propitious, as Job then thought to be his case, than hell and death. Therefore, when he had run over the whole story of his misery, he says that the last act is confusion. And this is the end of those on whom God lays His hand. For there is death in his anger, and life in his mercy! This is not inelegantly stated by Ecclesiasticus when he says, (Ecclesiasticus 37:28) "The life of a man is in the number of his days, but the days of Israel are innumerable." But as the authority of that writer is doubtful, let us leave him, and listen to a prophet, admirably teaching the same thing, in his own words, (Psalm 102:24,)

"He hath broken my strength in its course, he hath shortened my days: but I said, O Lord, take me not away in the midst of my days. Thy years are eternal. Heaven and earth, which thou didst found of old, shall perish; like a vesture shall they be folded up."

Thus far he has shewn how fleeting and frail the condition of man is, and how nothing under the heavens is stable, seeing they too are verging on destruction. He afterwards adds,

"But thou art, and thy years shall not end. The sons of thy servants shall dwell, and their posterity shall be established before thee." (Psalm 102:27, 28.)

We here see how he connects the salvation of the righteous with the eternity of God. As often, therefore, as they bring forward Job, afflicted by the hand of God and almost desperate, representing that nothing is left to him but death and the grave, I will answer, that while God is angry, this is the only end that awaits us, and that His mercy consists in rescuing us from the jaws of death.

The *fourth* passage is, (Job 34:14,)

"If He will direct his heart to him, he will draw the spirit and breath of man to himself; at the same time all flesh shall fail, and man shall return to ashes."

If these words are understood of the judgment, as if it were said, that by His anger man is dissolved, cut down, confounded, and brought to nothing, I will grant them more than they ask. If they understand that *the spirit,* that is, *the soul,* at death returns to God, and that *the breath,* (*flatus,*) that is, the power of motion or the vital action, withdraws from man, I have no objection. If they contend that the soul perishes, I oppose them strenuously, although the meaning of the Hebrew is somewhat different. But, contented with disposing of their cavils, I will not pursue the matter farther.

They brandish some other darts, but they are pointless, They give no stroke, and they do not even cause much fear. For they quote some passages which, besides being irrelevant, are taken from books of doubtful authority, as the 4th of Esdras, and the 2d of the Maccabees. To these, the answer we gave in discoursing of the Resurrection is sufficient. In one thing their procedure is shameless, and is seen by all to be so, namely, in claiming Esdras, though he is wholly on our side. And they are not ashamed to bring forward the books of the Maccabees, where dead Jeremiah prays to the Lord on behalf of his warring people; and where prayers are made for the dead, that they may be delivered from their sins! Possibly they have other arguments, but they are unknown to me, as it has not been my lot to see all their fictions. I have not intentionally omitted anything which might mislead, or make any impression on the simple.

I again desire all my readers, if I shall have any, to remember that the Catabaptists (whom, as embodying all kinds of abominations, it is sufficient to have named) are the authors of this famous dogma. Well may we suspect anything that proceeds from such a forge — a forge which has already fabricated, and is daily fabricating, so many monsters.

ROMANS ROAD TO SALVATION

I. Romans 3:10	As it is written, there is none righteous, no, not one.
II. Romans 3:23	For all have sinned, and come short of the glory of God.
III. Romans 5:8	But God commendeth his love toward us, in that, while we were yet sinners, Christ died for us.
IV. Romans 5:12	Wherefore, as by one man sin entered into the world, and death by sin; and so death passed upon all men, for that all have sinned.
V. Romans 6:23	For the wages of sin is death; but the gift of God is eternal life through Jesus Christ our Lord.
VI. Romans 10:9-11	That if thou shalt confess with thy mouth the Lord Jesus, and shalt believe in thine heart that God hath raised him from the dead, thou shalt be saved. For with the heart man believeth unto righteousness; and with the mouth confession is made unto salvation. For the scripture saith, whosoever believeth on him shall not be ashamed.
VII. Romans 10:13	For whosoever shall call upon the name of the Lord shall be saved.

Printed in the United States
99452LV00006B/22-24/A

9 781933 899435